THE ANALECTS

Other translations by David Hinton

Mencius

Chuang Tzu: The Inner Chapters

The Late Poems of Meng Chiao

The Selected Poems of Li Po

Landscape Over Zero *(Poems by Bei Dao)*

Forms of Distance *(Poems by Bei Dao)*

The Selected Poems of T'ao Ch'ien

The Selected Poems of Tu Fu

月顏氏聖心念嬰家居魯親里并宦遲

旦仁聞君居權敬味濟畏瑗

抒玄汙以梁水昔符海鍾

逵立禮器樂往之昔待鍾齊瑟

臬秋立禮虛世禮樂陵

月貲韋元百主改官

THE ANALECTS

Confucius

Translated by David Hinton

COUNTERPOINT WASHINGTON, D.C.

Library of Congress Cataloging-in-Publication Data
Confucius.
   [Lun yü.   English]
The Analects of Confucius / translated by David Hinton.
      p.   cm.
   Includes bibliographical references.
      I. Hinton, David, 1954– . II. Title.
PL2478.L36   1998
181'.112—dc21   98–39929
                           CIP

ISBN 1-887178-63-5 (alk. paper)

Printed in the United States of America on acid-free
paper that meets the American National Standards
Institute Z39-48 Standard.

Illustration: *Li-ch'i Stele at Confucius' Tomb,* Anonymous
(2nd C.). Ink rubbing. Courtesy of the Tokyo National
Museum.

Design and electronic production by David Bullen

COUNTERPOINT
P.O. Box 65793
Washington, D.C. 20035-5793

Counterpoint is a member of the Perseus Books Group.

10 9 8 7 6 5 4 3 2 1

FIRST PRINTING

Contents

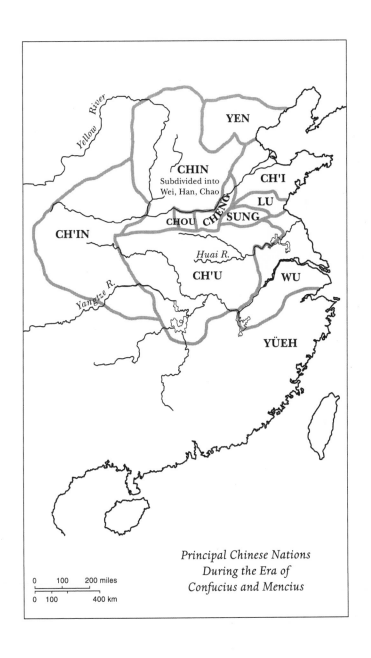

Yellow River

YEN

CHIN
Subdivided into
Wei, Han, Chao

CH'I

LU

CH'IN

CHOU CHENG SUNG

Huai R.

CH'U

WU

Yangtze R.

YÜEH

Principal Chinese Nations
During the Era of
Confucius and Mencius

0   100   200 miles

0   100   400 km

Introduction

Asked by a disciple if he should pray for him, a dying Confucius summed up: "My life has been my prayer" (7.35). Although Confucius (551–479 B.C.E.) was to become the most influential sage in human history, his had been a disappointing life indeed, for he had taken as his task the creation of a society in which everyone's life is a prayer. Needless to say, he failed miserably. But he did create the outline of such a society in his social philosophy, and it has survived as China's social ideal ever since, however rarely that ideal has been approached in actual practice. Formulated in the ruins of a magisterial monotheism, a situation not entirely unlike our own, his ideal represents the end of a devastating, millennium-long transformation from a spiritualist to a humanist culture. It recognized society as a structure of human relationships, and spoke of those relationships as a system of "ritual" that people enact in their daily lives, thus infusing the secular with sacred dimensions. The spoken realm of Confucius' teachings is occupied with the practical issues of how society works as a selfless weave of caring relationships; and in the unspoken realm, that ritual weave is extended into the vast primal ecology of a self-generating and harmonious cosmos. This body of thought, still remarkably current and even innovative, survives here in *The Analects,* a collection of aphoristic sayings that has had a deeper impact on more people's lives over a longer period of time than any other book in human history.

The tangible beginnings of Chinese civilization lie in the archaic Shang Dynasty (c. 1766–1040 B.C.E.), which bridged the transition from Neolithic to Bronze Age culture. (For an outline of the early dynasties and rulers that figure prominently in *The Analects,* see Historical Table.) The Shang was preceded by the Neolithic Hsia Dynasty, about which very little is known. It appears that in the Paleolithic cultures that preceded the Hsia, nature deities were worshiped as tribal ancestors: hence a tribe may have traced its lineage back to an originary "High Ancestor River," for instance. This practice apparently continued through the Hsia into the Shang, where evidence of it appears in oracle-bone inscriptions. Eventually, although these nature deities continued to be worshiped in their own right, religious life focused on the worship of human ancestors. By forging this religious system into a powerful form of theocratic government, the Shang was able to dominate China for no less than seven hundred years.

The Shang Emperors ruled by virtue of their lineage, which was sanctified by Shang Ti ("Celestial Lord"), a supreme deity who functioned as the source of creation, order, ethics, etc. (*Shang* here represents two entirely different words in Chinese.) The Shang lineage may even have led to Shang Ti as its originary ancestor. In any case, Shang Ti provided the Shang rulers with a transcendental source of legitimacy and power: he protected and advanced their interests, and through their spirit-ancestors, they could decisively influence Shang Ti's shaping of events. All aspects of people's lives were thus controlled by the Emperor: weather, harvest, politics, economics, religion, etc. Indeed, people didn't experience themselves as substantially different from spirits, for the human realm was simply an extension of the spirit realm.

Such was the imperial ideology, convenient to the uses of power, as it accorded little ethical value to the masses not of select lineages. (Not surprisingly, the rise of Shang Ti seems to coincide with the rise of the Shang Dynasty, and later myth speaks of him as the creator of Shang civilization.) In the cruelest of ironies, it was overwhelming physical suffering that brought the Chinese people into their earthly lives, beginning the transformation of this spiritualistic culture to a humanistic one. In the cultural legend, the early Shang rulers were paradigms of nobility and benevolence. But by the end of the Shang, the rulers had become cruel and tyrannical, and as there was no ethical system separate from the religious system, there was nothing to shield the people from their depredations. Meanwhile, a small nation was being pushed to the borders of the Shang realm by western tribes. This state of semi-barbarian people, known as the Chou, gradually adopted the cultural traits of the Shang. Eventually, under the leadership of the legendary sage-emperors Wen ("cultured") and Wu ("martial"), the Chou overthrew the tyrannical Shang ruler, thus founding the Chou Dynasty (1122–221), which was welcomed wholeheartedly by the Shang people.

The Chou conquerors were faced with an obvious problem: if the Shang lineage had an absolute claim to rule the world, how could the Chou justify replacing it with their own, and how could they legitimize their rule in the eyes of the Shang people? Their solution was to reinvent Shang Ti as *Heaven,* thus ending the Shang's claim to legitimacy by lineage, and then proclaim that the right to rule depended upon the Mandate of Heaven: once a ruler becomes unworthy, Heaven withdraws its mandate and bestows it on another. This was a major event in Chinese philosophy: the first investment of power with an ethical imperative. And happily, the early centuries of the Chou appear to have fulfilled that imperative admirably.

But eventually, the Chou foundered both because of its increasing inhumanity and its lack of the Shang's transcendent source of legitimacy: if the Mandate could be transferred to the Chou, it could obviously be transferred again. The rulers of the empire's component states (*chu hou:* "august lords") grew increasingly powerful, claiming more and more sovereignty over their lands, until finally they were virtually independent nations. Eventually these rulers (properly entitled "dukes") even began assuming the title of Emperor, thus equating themselves with the Chou Emperor, who was by now a mere figurehead. The rulers of these autonomous states could at least claim descent from those who were first given the territories by the early Chou rulers. But this last semblance of legitimacy was also crumbling because these rulers were frequently at war with one another, which hardly inspired confidence in the claim that they were familial members of the ruling kinship hierarchy that was sanctioned by Heaven. But more importantly, power was being usurped by a second tier of "august lords" whenever they had the strength to take it, and even a third tier of high government officials. In *The Analects*, we see this process primarily in Lu, Confucius' homeland, where the first tier of "august lords" takes the form of the Lu ruling family: Duke Chao (r. 541–509), Duke Ting (r. 509–495), and Duke Ai (r. 494–468). The second tier was the Three Families (Chi, Meng, and Shu), led by the patriarchs of the House of Chi, who had effectively usurped control of the state and set up their own governmental structure. And the rising third tier was made up of the ministers and regents of those Three Families, who had gained control of land and power and begun to challenge the families' dominance. This history, beginning with the Chou's overthrow of the Shang, represents a geologic split in China's social structure: political power was breaking free of its family / religious context and becoming a separate entity.

The final result of the Chou's "metaphysical" breakdown was, not surprisingly, all too physical: war. In addition to constant pressure from barbarians in the north (the first devastating blow to Chou power was a barbarian invasion in 770) and the Ch'u realm that dominated southern China, there was relentless fighting between the empire's component states and frequent rebellion within them. This internal situation, devastating to the people, continued to deteriorate after Confucius' time, until it finally gave an entire age its name: the Warring States Period (403–221). Meanwhile, rulers caught up in this ruthless competition began looking for the most able men to help them govern their states, and this precipitated the rise of an independent intellectual class – a monumental event, for this class constituted the first open space in the cultural framework from which the imperial ideology could be challenged.

The old social order had now collapsed entirely, and these

intellectuals began struggling to create a new one. Although this was one of the most virulent and chaotic periods in Chinese history, it was also the golden age of Chinese philosophy, for there were a "Hundred Schools of Thought" trying to envision what this new social order should be like. These schools were founded by thinkers who wandered the country with their disciples, teaching and trying to convince the various rulers to put their ideas into practice, for the desperate times had given them an urgent sense of political mission.

Confucius was the first great figure in this independent intellectual class and China's first self-conscious philosopher who can be historically verified in any sense. As with most intellectual figures in ancient China, very little is known of Confucius' life. But the essential outline of that life took on mythic proportions as the archetypal example of the Confucian Way: Through his devotion to self-cultivation, Confucius made himself into a great sage and devoted himself passionately to the public good in spite of hardships such as hunger, homelessness, unemployment, and life-threatening violence.

Confucius was born in Lu, where the Chou cultural tradition was especially strong, to a family that had once been part of the Shang aristocracy. So he was very conscious of inheriting both Shang and Chou cultures, and he never stopped looking to the golden eras of those dynasties for his models of human society, though his was a selective and idealized version of that past. Confucius' Chinese name was K'ung Ch'iu or K'ung Chung-ni, and he is known as K'ung Tzu or K'ung Fu-tzu, meaning "Master K'ung." It is from the second of these honorary names, K'ung Fu-tzu, that the latinized *Confucius* derives. Although his family technically belonged to the literate aristocracy, it had been reduced to very humble means some generations earlier, after its migration from a neighboring state where it had apparently lost favor with the rulers. So he was born to the literate class, but independent of the usual ties that class had to ruling interests – an unusual family situation which anticipated exactly the situation of the independent intellectual class he did so much to establish.

Confucius devoted himself to studies at a young age and perhaps held a number of menial government positions. But such a brilliant and outspoken character was surely not welcome in government, so Confucius pursued his political mission as a teacher of men (not surprisingly, this was an utterly sexist culture) who aspired to government service. In this capacity he was widely admired, and his students were eagerly sought as the various rulers knew them to be the best-trained men in the empire – a cruel irony, for this meant that most of the prominent disciples became high officials serving the very families Confucius detested because they were undermining society by usurping power. In his late forties, Confucius took the first of several significant government positions in Lu, the highest of which was Minister of Justice. But at the age of fifty-six, realizing that his Way would always be ignored there, Confucius left Lu and spent thirteen years traveling from state to state advising rulers, hoping his ideas would be put into practice and so lead to a more humane society. Although he was known and respected as a sage by a number of the rulers he visited, none showed any inclination to employ him or enact his ideas. Utterly disappointed at his failure to have any real political impact, he finally returned home in his late sixties and devoted himself to teaching and establishing the classic texts that preserved the ancient cultural tradition.

Our primary surviving source for the teachings of Confucius is the *Lun Yü: The Analects,* or more literally, "The Selected Sayings." The book's defining characteristic is its aphoristic form: it is a collage of brief aphoristic fragments, each appearing with little supporting context. This lack of systematic precision extends to the language as well, for there was little sense of a precise philosophical language prior to Confucius. In the effort to articulate his ideas, Confucius was borrowing older terms and reshaping their meanings. Indeed, the Confucian philosophical world can be outlined by defining a small constellation of such terms (see Key Terms), but in most cases their meanings shift each time they are used and so remain somewhat obscure. So rather than systematically developing a philosophical system, the book attains its sense of coherence through a process of accretion.

The difficulties posed by the text itself are complicated by the question of authenticity. A good share of the book's fragments are assumed to represent the Master's teachings, handed down accurately by his disciples, but a great many clearly do not. Numerous versions of the Master's sayings were edited over the course of centuries, a time when the concept of individual authorship had not been firmly established, and much extraneous material was included by various editors, sometimes with the apparent intent of smuggling their preferred ideas into the canonical text. Although most of these fragments add depth and complexity to the text, some contradict its overall spirit. It is also clear that very little of what the Master said was recorded, and a great deal of what was recorded was not included in *The Analects* we now have: Mencius (4th c. B.C.E.) often cites the Master, for instance, and most of those citations are not included in *The Analects*. But for all the concerns about how authentic the text is and how accurately or thoroughly it portrays the historical Confucius' thought, *The Analects* still possesses an impressive stylistic unity and represents, as a matter of historical fact, the fundamental body of thought that has shaped Chinese civilization for over two thousand years.

Confucius' social philosophy derives from a rational empiricism, a methodology which represents a total break with Shang spiritualism, and this is perhaps why it has proven so enduring. Blatant power politics had made it impossible to believe in Heaven (let alone Shang Ti) as a transcendental source of order and legitimacy, so he tried to rescue the fragmented Chou culture by putting it on a more viable rational and secular basis. Confucius developed a social philosophy from the empirical observation that human society is a structure, a weave of relationships between individuals who each occupy a certain locus in that structure: parent and child, ruler and subject, friend and friend, merchant and customer, and so forth. Confucius invested this anthropological insight with a philosophical dimension by recognizing that a healthy community depends upon an attitude of human caring among its members – most especially its government, which should nurture first, teach second, and only then govern. Always looking to the past as his source of wisdom, Confucius saw that societies flourished when their citizens (their rulers above all) honored this moral principle, and inevitably crumbled when they ignored it: even the powerful transcendental glue of the Shang theocracy couldn't withstand the corrosive influence of the Shang Emperors' depredations.

But Confucius' social philosophy goes well beyond this moral dimension, for he described the web of social responsibilities as a system of "Ritual" (*li*: see Key Terms). *Ritual* is a crucial instance of how Confucius forged a philosophy by reshaping certain key terms, for it had been a religious concept associated with the worship of spirits. The spiritualist regime that had dominated China since the rise of the Shang had crumbled. Although Confucius recognized sacrifices to the spirit-world, he didn't necessarily believe any of the religious claims associated with such worship. For him, the value of such practices lay in the function they served in the Ritual structure of society. (This suggests an explanation for Confucius' oft-noted refusal to speak of the spirit-realm: to affirm the reality of that realm would be duplicitous, and to deny it would undermine the Ritual efficacy of practices associated with it.) It was in this context that Confucius extended the use of Ritual to include all the caring acts by which we fulfill our responsibilities to others in the community – hence the entire weave of everyday social life takes on the numinous aspect of the sacred.

This is a society in which individual identity is defined entirely in terms of the community. There is little sense of the inner self in *The Analects:* the Ritual social fabric is paramount, and individual identity is defined entirely in terms of a person's social roles. All of the Confucian moral virtues (see Key Terms) apply only in the social context: one cannot speak of a person being virtuous in isolation. And there is indeed a kind of spiritual clarity in the selflessness of this Ritual weave, a clarity that became a defining aspect in the structure of Chinese political and spiritual consciousness throughout the ages.

As it has shaped Chinese society for millennia, one must assume this Confucian system has proven useful to those in power. Confucius was struggling to describe this Ritual structure, so he naturally emphasized the individual's social role. This led to the appearance of an undue emphasis on the proper behavior of subordinates, and this is the aspect of Confucian thought that has proven so appealing to the interests of power. The brand of Confucianism wielded throughout the centuries as power's ideology of choice focused on select ideas involving selfless submission to authority: parental, political, masculine, historic, textual. And the "sacred" Ritual dimensions of these hierarchical relationships only made them that much more oppressive. It is this aspect of the Confucian tradition that has become so problematic in modern times, for intellectuals came to recognize it as the force that was preventing China's modernization. But selfless submission plays little part in the thought of Confucius himself, and as his thought was modified over the centuries by thinkers and social forces, this aspect could very well have been replaced. Indeed, not long after Confucius' death, Mencius had already challenged these hierarchies with a fierce insistence on the responsibilities of those in power, even declaring the people more important than the ruler. Nevertheless, China's ruling interests have rarely concerned themselves with the egalitarian ideas so central to Confucius' thought: social justice, political dissent, the role of intellectuals as social critics.

For Confucius, the Ritual community depends upon these egalitarian elements, and they depend ultimately on the education and cultivation of the community members. To call Confucius' contribution in this regard epochal would be an understatement. He was China's first professional teacher, founding the idea of a broad moral education, and in addition, he established the classic texts that defined the essential content of that education. As if that weren't enough, he also established the enduring principle of egalitarian education – that all people should receive some form of education, that this is necessary for the health of a moral community. He focused his attention on the education of intellectuals, which was of necessity much more exhaustive than that of the masses, but he thought even this education should be available to any who seek it, however humble their origins. In fact, not only was the Master himself from a relatively humble background, but nearly all of his disciples were as well.

The purpose of such education and cultivation is to become a *chün-tzu,* a "noble-minded" one. And here again we find Confucius forging a philosophy by reshaping terminology. *Chün-tzu* had previously referred to those of noble birth, but Confucius redefined the term (and what it is to be noble) to mean those of talent and intellectual accomplishment. Here the application of Confucius' rational methodology to society resulted in a transformation of aristocracy to meritocracy, for government in Confucian society is a government of *chün-tzu,* a government of the high-minded rather than the high-born. To become government officials in China, candidates generally devoted themselves to many years of reflective study in order to pass daunting examinations, thereby proving they possessed formidable learning and moral insight. History thus replaces the spirit-realm as the source of knowledge about government and society, and this knowledge is recorded in books: it is the self-justifying and reasonable discoveries of past sages. Hence the wise man replaced the holy man, whose policy recommendations would have been dictated by oracle-bone divination. As a result of Confucius' legacy, Chinese culture has always had a reverence for learning that is perhaps deeper than in any other culture. And however often their role has been ignored or subverted by ruling interests, China has essentially always been a nation governed by philosophers.

The ideal of such a philosopher, the ideal result of the *chün-tzu*'s self-cultivation, is mastery of the *Tao* (Way). Tao originally meant "way," as in "pathway" or "roadway," but Confucius recast it to mean the effortless process of human society functioning according to its natural Ritual structure. This Confucian Tao shows a striking resemblance to the more familiar Tao of the ancient Taoist masters, who recast it as a spiritual concept by transforming it into a kind of ontological Way. For them, Tao is the ontological ground or process (hence, a "Way") from which the ten thousand things arise. In both cases, the term refers to a vast organic process. And in both cases, mastery of the Way involves understanding how to dwell as an integral part of that process. For Confucius, the most exemplary masters of the Way were ancient sage-rulers who led societies in which this Ritual process of *li* functioned effortlessly. Their actions were spontaneous and selfless, for the ruler was simply the ruler: his actions followed directly from his Ritual role in the community, so he himself "did nothing":

> If anyone has managed to rule by doing nothing
> (wu-wei), surely it was Shun. And how did he do so
> much by doing nothing? He just sat reverently facing
> south, that's all! (XV.5)

Wu-wei is a central concept in Taoism, where it is associated with *tzu-jan*, the mechanism of the Tao's process. *Tzu-jan*'s literal meaning is "self-so" or "the of-itself" or "being such of itself," hence "spontaneous" or "natural." But a more descriptive translation might be "occurrence appearing of itself," for it is meant to describe the ten thousand things unfolding spontaneously, each according to its own nature. For Taoists, we dwell as an organic part of *tzu-jan* by practicing *wu-wei*, which literally means "nothing doing," or more descriptively, "selfless action": acting as a spontaneous part of *tzu-jan* rather than with self-conscious intention. Here in its sole appearance in *The Analects*, *wu-wei* functions in much the same way. But rather than making us a part of *tzu-jan*, the Confucian practice of *wu-wei* makes us a part of *tzu-jan*'s Confucian counterpart: *li* (Ritual). Shun has so mastered the Way that he need only sit facing south, the ceremonial position of the Emperor, and the Ritual weave of human community thereby continues its self-generating process, a sacred process inspiring nothing less than reverence.

These structural similarities reflect a deeper unity in the

two systems of thought. This unity was explored in a most profound way by the thinkers of a philosophical movement known as DarkEnigma Learning (Hsüan Hsüeh), which arose in the third and fourth centuries of the current era and explored the dark and enigmatic regions of ontology. There they discovered a fundamental unity in Confucian and Taoist thought when they recognized that Confucius located his human society within a cosmology that the Taoists described eloquently, but which he himself referred to only through silence:

> Adept Kung said: "When the Master talks about
> civility and cultivation, you can hear what he says.
> But when he talks about the nature of things and the
> Way of Heaven, you can't hear a word." (V.12)

"Heaven" is a major component in that shared cosmology, and a particularly significant instance of Confucius developing ideas through terminology. The most primitive meaning of *Heaven (T'ien)* is "sky." By extension, it also comes to mean "transcendence," for our most primal sense of transcendence may be the simple act of looking up into the sky. So it's hardly surprising that when the Chou wanted to reinvent Shang Ti in a more impersonal form, they would choose Heaven. By association with the idea of transcendence and that which is beyond us, it is natural that *Heaven* also comes to mean "fate" or "destiny." And this is precisely what we find in Confucius, where "destiny" has evolved out of the early Chou sense of an impersonal deity. But rather than destiny in the sense of a transcendental force deciding human fate, this is destiny as the inevitable evolution of things according to the principles inherent to them. Although Confucius focuses on its manifestations in human history, there is little real difference between this Confucian Heaven and that of the Taoists, who identified it with the natural process of *tzu-jan*. Confucius even goes so far as to say that the most profound level of his teachings is the silent voice of Heaven's natural process:

> The Master said: "I'd love to just say nothing."
>
> "But if you say nothing," said Adept Kung, "how would we disciples hand down your teachings?"
>
> "What has Heaven ever said?" replied the Master. "The four seasons keep turning and the hundred things keep emerging – but what has Heaven ever said?" (17.17)

This sounds more like Lao Tzu than Confucius, at least until we realize that the Ritual structure of society is part of a much larger weave, the Ritual structure of natural process, a point made by Hsün Tzu (ca. 313–238 B.C.E.), one of the most important early developers of Confucian philosophy:

> Through Ritual, Heaven and earth join in harmony, sun and moon shine, the four seasons proceed in order, the stars and constellations march, the rivers flow, and all

things flourish; men's likes and dislikes are regulated and their joys and hates made appropriate. Those below are obedient and those above are enlightened; all things change but do not become disordered . . . .

(*Hsün Tzu,* trans. Watson, p. 94)

Hence, our initial definition of the Confucian Tao ("the effortless process of human society functioning according to its natural Ritual structure") can be dramatically expanded, making it comparable to the Taoist Tao: "the effortless process of the cosmos functioning according to its natural Ritual structure." This Ritual process of the cosmos never falters, and so it is unproblematic. This is no doubt why Confucius is so unconcerned with it. Instead he focuses his attention on human society, where this Ritual process can so easily fail. So for a society to abide by the Tao means it functions as an organic part of the cosmological process. Here is the probable explanation for why Confucius sometimes speaks of Heaven as if it were a cosmic moral will sustaining the human order: the Ritual structure of the cosmos is a self-generating normative order, so it has the natural urge to restore itself when it is disrupted in the human realm.

It would seem the difference between *li* and *tzu-jan* is a matter of emphasis: while *tzu-jan* emphasizes individual things evolving in a system according to their own nature, *li* emphasizes a system evolving through individuals according to its own nature. But in both cases, it is a dynamic system of complex interrelationships that is being described. The difference in emphasis reflects the overall difference between Confucian and Taoist thought: the Confucian emphasizes community and the Taoist emphasizes individuals. These two Ways are traditionally described as the two poles of Chinese thought, but their shared cosmology affords them a fundamental unity, and that unity is no doubt why Chinese culture could eventually adopt both of these Ways simultaneously: the Confucian Way has defined the societal realm for Chinese intellectuals throughout the millennia, and the Way of philosophical Taoism has defined the private spiritual realm.

DarkEnigma Learning traced this fundamental unity to the deepest regions of cosmology: to nonbeing, the primal emptiness from which the ten thousand transformations issue forth according to the principles of *tzu-jan* and *li*. Mindful of Lao Tzu's famous dictum "Those who know don't speak, and those who speak don't know," DarkEnigma Learning held that Lao Tzu and Chuang Tzu hadn't yet fully identified themselves with nonbeing, so they spoke of it at length because it was something outside themselves, something in which they were still deficient. Confucius, on the other hand, was completely identified with nonbeing, and so knew how utterly beyond words it is. He therefore spoke only of being, though it is true he does indicate how essential such identification with the emptiness of nonbeing is for a true sage, as when he speaks of understanding "through dark silence" (VII.2), or in this description of Yen Hui, his favorite and most accomplished disciple: "Yen Hui's nearly made it: He's almost always empty" (XI.19). Indeed, it may well be that this identification with nonbeing is the epitome of Ritual selflessness.

Given the precision and depth of his subtle references to the cosmology that frames his social philosophy, it seems likely that cosmology played a larger role in Confucius' thought than the surviving record indicates. But even if we had more of his statements in this area, the motif of silence would no doubt remain dominant. Indeed, silence may be the most resounding instance of Confucius crafting a philosophy by crafting a terminology. Whether or not he was in fact identified with nonbeing, this silence was possible for him because he wasn't struggling to create a cosmology. In his social philosophy, he seems instead to be drawing out the implications of a cosmology that already existed in the culture. Rather than a newly created replacement for the Shang monotheism, it had apparently survived from the more primal cultures that preceded the Shang, thus revealing the Shang monotheism as a mere ideological overlay convenient to the uses of power. The resilience of this cosmology after a thousand years of neglect suggests the possibility that such a cosmology may yet reemerge in the West, especially as it is so consistent with the modern scientific account of the cosmos. We have certainly witnessed the same kind of catastrophic cultural collapse in this last century as China did in Confucius' time, and the insights that emerged so long ago from China's similar experience could well play a significant role in whatever renewal may take place here over the next millennium. For this to happen, it is clear that the hierarchical Ritual relationships of Confucianism must be replaced by egalitarian ones, but there is no structural reason why this cannot happen. In any case, the cosmology that shaped Chinese civilization was a resurgence of an ancient cosmology, a return to the culture's most primal roots – the Paleolithic and beyond. It is a primal realm where the categories of secular and sacred dissolve, where everything and nothing is sacred.

It was Confucius' great achievement to articulate a viable human order that is empirically consistent with the existential verities of that cosmology. In so doing, he combined a rational humanistic conceptual world with a primal organismic cosmos: rationality as a perfectly natural outgrowth of the self-generating cosmos. The Ritual society, a dynamic of relationships, is a kind of human ecology, and it is woven into the vast natural ecology of cosmological process. The spiritual ecology of this shared cosmology might also be seen as a return to the original spirituality of paleolithic China, for the sense of belonging to natural process is a secular version of the worship of nature deities as ancestral spirits.

What distinguishes the human from other manifestations of this cosmos is its particular ecology: people literally make themselves human by fulfilling the responsibilities inherent to their position in the Ritual weave, thereby strengthening the social community. Indeed, the central word that Confucius used to describe a person who masterfully fulfills the responsibilities of Ritual, who dwells as an integral part of the Ritual weave of society, is *jen* (*Humanity:* see Key Terms), a term he broadened to mean a selfless and reverent concern for the well-being of others, but which retained its original meaning as the verbal form of the noun meaning a human. This complex of meanings appears visually in the paired elements in its graph, "human" and "two": 仁. Hence the social aspect of being human. So to observe Ritual, to dwell as an integral part of the Ritual weave of society is to be, by definition, human. And conversely, to violate that Ritual weave is to be inhuman, for when that is violated the human ecology threatens to unravel. And this principle might be extended to the full cosmological dimensions of Ritual: to dwell as an integral part of the Ritual weave of the cosmos is to be human in the most elemental sense; and conversely, to violate that Ritual weave is to be inhuman in the most elemental sense, for when that is violated the natural ecology threatens to unravel.

So it is that Confucius established the human community in intimate contact with natural process and its ontological source in nonbeing, an intimacy that is perhaps the most characteristic and profound aspect in the deep structure of Chinese consciousness: a kind of spiritual ecology that seems to have been there from the beginning in the organic, open-form structure of the language itself, and which eventually became central to Taoist and Ch'an (Zen) Buddhist practices, as well as all the major art forms. The three regions of this cosmology appear almost schematically in countless Chinese landscape paintings, for instance: the pregnant emptiness of nonbeing; the natural process of being in its constant burgeoning forth from nonbeing; and finally, within that natural process, the human. And with their sparsely peopled landscapes so dramatically burgeoning forth out of vast realms of emptiness, such paintings do indeed render a majestic vision: human community nestled in the primal ecology of a spontaneously self-generating and harmonious cosmos.

肖顏樂迁是十
氏聖立扵仁元
　心禮玄聞
賚念器浮君
真樂水同
鷹廷注權
世普水敬
親禮晉濟思
里樂鍾海懷
并陵馨
官遲理

1   To Learn, and Then

1   The Master said: "To learn, and then, in its due season, put what you have learned into practice – isn't that still a great pleasure? And to have a friend visit from somewhere far away – isn't that still a great joy? When you're ignored by the world like this, and yet bear no resentment – isn't that great nobility?"

2   Master Yu[1] said: "It's honoring parents and elders that makes people human. Then they rarely turn against authority. And if people don't turn against authority, they never rise up and pitch the country into chaos.

"The noble-minded cultivate roots. When roots are secure, the Way is born. To honor parents and elders – isn't that the root of Humanity?"[2]

3   The Master said: "Clever words and sanctimonious looks: in such people, Humanity is rare indeed."

4   Master Tseng[3] said: "Each day I ask three things of myself: Have I been trustworthy in all that I've done for other people? Have I stood by my words[4] in dealing with friends? Have I practiced all that I've been taught?"

5   The Master said: "To show the Way for a nation of a thousand war-chariots, a ruler pays reverent attention to the country's affairs and always stands by his words. He maintains economy and simplicity, always loving the people, and so employs the people only in due season."

6   The Master said: "In youth, respect your parents when home and your elders when away. Think carefully before you speak, and stand by your words. Love the whole expanse of things, and make an intimate of Humanity. Then, if you have any energy left, begin cultivating yourself."

7   Adept Hsia[5] said: "Cherishing wisdom as if it were a beautiful woman, devoting their strength to serving parents and their lives to serving a ruler, standing by their words in dealing with friends – such people may say they've never studied, but I would call them learned indeed."

8 The Master said: "If you're grave and thoughtful, people look to you with the veneration due a noble. And if you're learned, too, you're never inflexible.

"Above all else, be loyal and stand by your words. Never befriend those who are not kindred spirits. And when you're wrong, don't be afraid to change."

9 Master Tseng said: "Be thorough in mourning parents, and meticulous in the ancestral sacrifices, then the people's Integrity[6] will return to its original fullness."

10 Adept Ch'in asked of Adept Kung:[7] "Whenever the Master visits a country, he learns all about its government. Does he have to search out this information, or is it just given to him?"

Adept Kung replied: "Congenial, good-natured, reverent, frugal, deferential – that's how he learns so much. It's altogether different from the way others inquire, don't you think?"

11 The Master said: "Consider your plans when your father is alive, then see what you do when he dies. If you

leave your father's Way unchanged for all three years of mourning, you are indeed a worthy child."

12   Master Yu said: "The most precious fruit of Ritual is harmony. The Way of the ancient Emperors found its beauty in this, and all matters great and small depend upon it.

"Still, things go wrong. You may understand this harmony and even instill things with it, but if you fail to shape harmony with Ritual, you'll never make things right."

13   Master Yu said:

> *"Make standing by words your Duty,*[8]
> *and your words will last and last,*
>
> *make reverence an everyday Ritual,*
> *and you'll stay clear of all disgrace –*
>
> *then kindred spirits remain kindred,*
> *and you're worthy to be their ancestor."*

14   The Master said: "The noble-minded are content without a full belly or the comforts of home; they're quick

in action but cautious in word; they rectify themselves by seeking out a master of the Way. And so they can be called lovers of learning."

15   Adept Kung said: *"When poor, never fawning; when rich, never arrogant.* How does that sound?"

The Master replied: "Not bad. But not so good as *When poor, delighting in the Way; when rich, devoted to Ritual.*"

Adept Kung said: "In *The Book of Songs,* the noble-minded are perfected

> *as if cut, as if polished,*
> *as if carved, as if burnished.*[9]

Is that what you mean?"

The Master replied: "Only with a person like you can I even begin to talk about the *Songs.* When they tell you about the past, you understand the future."

16   The Master said: "Don't grieve when people fail to recognize your ability. Grieve when you fail to recognize theirs."

月　顏　皋　迁　身
　　氏　立　抒　仁
聖　心　禮　玄　聞
念　器　污　君
希　真　樂　以　同
家　世　之　注　權
元　魯　普　敬
興　親　禮　待
百　里　樂　鍾　思
其　并　陵　磬
改　官　遲　理

1   The Master said: "In government, the secret is Integrity. Use it, and you'll be like the polestar: always dwelling in its proper place, the other stars turning reverently about it."

2   The Master said: "There are three hundred songs in *The Book of Songs,* but this one phrase tells it all: *thoughts never twisty.*"[1]

3   The Master said: "If you use government to show them the Way and punishment to keep them true, the people will grow evasive and lose all remorse. But if you use Integrity to show them the Way and Ritual to keep them true, they'll cultivate remorse and always see deeply into things."

4   The Master said: "At fifteen I devoted myself to learning, and at thirty stood firm. At forty I had no doubts,

and at fifty understood the Mandate of Heaven. At sixty I listened in effortless accord. And at seventy I followed the mind's passing fancies without overstepping any bounds."

5   When Lord Meng Yi[2] asked about honoring parents, the Master said: "Never disobey."

Later, when Fan Ch'ih[3] was driving his carriage, the Master said: "Meng asked me about honoring parents, and I said *Never disobey.*"

"What did you mean by that?" asked Fan Ch'ih.

"In life, serve them according to Ritual," replied the Master. "In death, bury them according to Ritual. And then, make offerings to them according to Ritual."

6   When Lord Meng Yi's son, Wu-po, asked about honoring parents, the Master replied: "The only time you should cause your mother and father to worry is when you are sick."

7   When Adept Yu[4] asked about honoring parents, the Master said: "These days, being a worthy child just

means keeping parents well-fed. That's what we do for dogs and horses. Everyone can feed their parents – but without reverence, they may as well be feeding animals."

8   When Adept Hsia asked about honoring parents, the Master said: "It's the way you do things that matters. When there's work, children may make it easy for their parents. And when there's wine and food, they may serve their parents first. But isn't there more to honoring parents than this?"

9   The Master said: "I can talk with Yen Hui[5] all day, and he never disagrees. He seems like a fool. But thinking about how he is when alone, I realize that he reveals my most essential principles. Hui is no fool."

10   The Master said: "If you look at their intentions, examine their motives, and scrutinize what brings them contentment – how can people hide who they are? How can they hide who they really are?"

11 The Master said: "If you can revive the ancient and use it to understand the modern, then you're worthy to be a teacher."

12 The Master said: "A noble-minded man is not an implement."

13 Adept Hsia asked about the noble-minded, and the Master said: "Such people act before they speak, then they speak according to their actions."

14 The Master said: "The noble-minded are all-encompassing, not stuck in doctrines. Little people are stuck in doctrines."

15 The Master said: "To learn and never think – that's delusion. But to think and never learn – that is perilous indeed!"

16   The Master said: "Devote yourself to strange doctrines and principles, and there's sure to be pain and suffering."

17   The Master said: "Shall I explain understanding for you, Lu? When you understand something, know that you understand it. When you don't understand something, know that you don't understand it. That's understanding."

18   Adept Chang was studying, hoping for rewards. The Master said: "Listen to all that you can – then, if you forget the deficiencies and speak about the rest cautiously, you'll avoid trouble. See all that you can – then, if you forget the perilous and act upon the rest cautiously, you'll avoid regret. In speech avoid trouble, in action avoid regret – then rewards will come of themselves."

19   Duke Ai[6] asked: "What must I do to make the people willing subjects?"

   "If you raise up the straight and cast out the crooked,"

replied Confucius, "the people will honor you. If you raise up the crooked and cast out the straight, they'll never honor you."

20   Lord Chi K'ang[7] asked how he could persuade the people to be reverent and loyal. The Master said: "Preside over them with solemn dignity, then the people will be reverent. Honor your parents and cherish your children, then the people will be loyal. Promote the worthy and instruct the feckless, then the people will be persuaded."

21   Someone asked Confucius: "Why aren't you in government?"

The Master replied: *"The Book of History says: Honor your parents, simply honor your parents and make your brothers friends – this too is good government.* That's really being in government, so why govern by serving in government?"

22   The Master said: "Unless you stand by your words, you'll never know what you're capable of. A large cart with no yoke-bar for the harness, a small cart with no collar-bar for the harness – what use are they?"

23 Adept Chang asked if we can know what will come ten generations from now. The Master replied: "The first of our dynasties was the Hsia. Although changes were made, the Hsia rituals were continued in the Shang, and so the Shang could be known. Although changes were made, the Shang rituals were continued in the Chou, and so the Chou could be known. Whatever follows our own Chou Dynasty, even if it comes a hundred generations from now, we can know it in the same way."

24 The Master said: "Sacrificing to the spirits of ancestors not your own is mere flattery. And to recognize a Duty without carrying it out is mere cowardice."

異頋月
立抒旦士
禮玄聞仁
器汙君
樂水同
注三耀
普水敬
待済
鍾海異
齋磬
遲

陟頋
心氏聖
念嬰家
真唇魯
慮世
禮親里
樂陵并
官
遲

東元輕百主禾改

III   Eight Rows of Dancers

1   Speaking of the Chi family patriarch, Confucius said: "Eight rows of dancers at his ancestral temple, as if he were an Emperor: If this can be endured, what can't be?"[1]

2   As they cleared sacrificial vessels from the temple, the Three Families sang the Yung hymn. The Master mimicked its words:

> *the great lords in attendance,*
> *the Emperor august and majestic,*[2]

then asked: "What has this to do with the temple of these Three Families?"

3   The Master said: "If you're human without Humanity, you know nothing of Ritual. If you're human without Humanity, you know nothing of music."

4   Lin Fang[3] asked about the root of Ritual. The Master replied: "What a huge question! In Ritual, simplicity rather than extravagance. In mourning, grief rather than repose."

5   The Master said: "Those wild tribes in the far north and east – they still honor their sovereigns. They're nothing like us: we Chinese have given up such things."

6   The Chi family patriarch went to perform the imperial sacrifice on T'ai Mountain. The master said to Jan Ch'iu:[4] "That is for Emperors alone to perform. Can't you save us from this?"

"No, I cannot," replied Jan Ch'iu.

"Ohhh," groaned the Master. "And how could the god of T'ai Mountain know even less than Lin Fang about such things?"

7   The Master said: "The noble-minded never contend. It's true that archery is a kind of contention. But even

then, they bow and yield to each other when stepping up to the range. And when they step down, they toast each other. Even in contention, they retain their nobility."

8   Adept Hsia asked: "What does it mean when the *Songs* say

> *Dimpled smile so entrancing,*
> *glancing eyes so full of grace:*
> *purest silk so ready for color?*"[5]

"For a painting," replied the Master, "you need a ground of pure silk."

"And for Ritual – what ground do you need?"

"How you've lifted my spirits, Hsia!" exclaimed the Master. "With you, I can truly discuss the *Songs!*"

9   The Master said: "I can speak of the Hsia Dynasty's rituals, though evidence is scarce among the Hsia's descendants in Ch'i. And I can speak of the Shang's rituals, though records and scholars are scarce among the Shang's descendants in Sung. Without such scarcity, I could prove what I say."

10   The Master said: "As for what follows the opening libation at the Imperial Sacrifice, I'd rather not see how they do it these days."

11   Someone asked about the theory of the Imperial Sacrifice. The Master replied: "I've never understood it. If there were someone who understood, he could reveal the workings of all beneath Heaven this easily," and he pointed a finger to the palm of his hand.

12   *Sacrifice as if present* means *Sacrifice to spirits as if the spirits were present.* So the Master said: "If I'm not there at my own ancestral sacrifice, it's as if there were no sacrifice at all."

13   Wang-sun Chia[6] inquired of the Master: "What does it mean to say

> *As for homage at the household shrine,*
> *homage pays better at the kitchen stove?"*

"That's wrong," responded the Master. "Once you've offended Heaven, there's nowhere to turn."

14 The Master said: "The Chou Dynasty looked to its predecessors, the Shang and Hsia. How elegant and majestic Chou culture was – and now, we follow the Chou."

15 When he was in the Grand Temple, the Master asked questions about everything he saw. Someone said: "Who says this son of a Tsou villager understands Ritual? When he was in the Grand Temple, he asked questions about everything he saw."

When he heard this, the Master said: "That questioning is itself Ritual."

16 The Master said: *"People's strength differs. So, in archery, shooting* through *the target-skin isn't the point.* That is the way of the ancients."

17 As the ceremony had fallen into neglect, Adept Kung wanted to do away with sacrificing sheep to announce a new moon to the ancestors. The Master said: "You love sheep, Kung, but I love Ritual."

18   The Master said: "If you make a Ritual of serving your sovereign, people will call it mere flattery."

19   Duke Ting[7] asked how the sovereign should employ ministers and how ministers should serve the sovereign. Confucius replied: "The sovereign should make employing ministers a matter of Ritual. And ministers should make serving their sovereign a matter of loyalty."

20   The Master said: "In the first of the *Songs*, there's joy without abandon and grief without laceration."

21   Duke Ai asked Tsai Yü[8] about altars to the earth god. Tsai Yü said: "The Hsia Dynasty used a pine grove. The Shang used cedar. And the Chou used chestnut, saying *Then the people will tremble like the chestnut in wind.*"

When he heard this, the Master said: "Never speak of what has already happened. Never criticize what has already run its course. Never condemn what is already done and gone."

22   The Master said: "Kuan Chung[9] was truly an implement of little use!"

Someone asked: "But wasn't Kuan Chung terribly frugal?"

"Kuan had three separate homes," replied the Master. "And his officers never did double duty. Is that frugal?"

"But still, Kuan Chung understood Ritual, didn't he?"

"A sovereign screens his gate with trees. But Kuan also built such a screen. After sovereigns meet and toast their friendship, they place the cups on a ceremonial stand. Kuan also had such a stand. If Kuan understood Ritual, who doesn't?"

23   When he was talking about music with the great music-master of Lu, the Master said: "This is what we can know of music: It begins in the sounds of harmony – then, pure and clear and unbroken, it swells into completion."

24   Asking to see the Master, a border-guard at Yi said: "Of all the noble-minded men who've traveled this way, none have declined to see me." So the disciples took him to see the Master.

As he was leaving, the border-guard said: "My friends,

CHAPTER III

why mourn what's been lost? The Way's been unknown everywhere under Heaven for a very long time, and Heaven's about to use your Master like the clapper in a bell."

25   The Master said Emperor Shun's[10] music was perfectly beautiful, and perfectly virtuous, too. He said Emperor Wu's[11] music was perfectly beautiful, but not perfectly virtuous.

26   The Master said: "Governing without generosity, Ritual without reverence, mourning without grief – how could I bear to see such things?"

月　顏　奧　迻　珤　仁　士
氏　立　禮　　　聞　元
心　禮　器　汙　君
念　樂　真　以　局　權
家　之　世　注　敬
希　魯　普　水　添
元　親　符　鍾　思
百　里　樂　陵
主　弄　齊
改　官　遲

IV   Of Villages, Humanity

1   The Master said: "Of villages, Humanity is the most beautiful. If you choose to dwell anywhere else, how can you be called wise?"

2   The Master said: "Without Humanity, you can't dwell in adversity for long, and you can't dwell in prosperity for long. If you're Humane, Humanity is your repose. And if you're wise, Humanity is your reward."

3   The Master said: "Only the Humane can love people, and only they can despise people."

4   The Master said: "Those who aspire to Humanity – they despise no one."

5   The Master said: "Wealth and position – that's what people want. But if you enjoy wealth and position

without following the Way, you'll never dwell at ease. Poverty and obscurity – that's what people despise. And if you endure poverty and obscurity without following the Way, you'll never get free.

"If you ignore Humanity, how will you gain praise and renown? The noble-minded don't forget Humanity for a single moment, not even in the crush of confusion and desperation."

6   The Master said: "I've never seen a person who really loves Humanity and despises Inhumanity. Those who love Humanity know of nothing more essential. And those who despise Inhumanity act with such Humanity that Inhumanity never touches them.

"Can people devote their full strength to Humanity for even a single day? I've never seen anyone who isn't strong enough. There may be such people, but I've never seen them."

7   The Master said: "A person's various faults are all of a piece. Recognizing your faults is a way of understanding Humanity."

8   The Master said: "If you hear the Way one morning and die that night, you die content."

9   The Master said: "Aspiring to the Way, but ashamed of bad clothes and bad food: such a person knows nothing worth discussing."

10   The Master said: "In their dealings with all beneath Heaven, the noble-minded do not themselves favor some things and oppose others. They form judgments according to Duty."

11   The Master said: "While the noble-minded cherish Integrity, little people cherish territory. And while the noble-minded cherish laws, little people cherish privilege."

12   The Master said: "If profit guides your actions, there will be no end of resentment."

13   The Master said: "If you can found a nation on Ritual and yielding, what more is there? If you cannot found a nation on Ritual and yielding, what's left of Ritual?"

14   The Master said: "Don't worry if you have no position: worry about making yourself worthy of one. Don't worry if you aren't known and admired: devote yourself to a life that deserves admiration."

15   The Master said: "Tseng! There's a single thread stringing my Way together."

"There is indeed," replied Master Tseng.

When the Master left, some disciples asked: "What did he mean?"

"Be loyal to the principles of your heart, and treat others with that same loyalty,"[1] answered Master Tseng. "That is the Master's Way. There is nothing more."

16   The Master said: "The noble-minded are clear about Duty. Little people are clear about profit."

17   The Master said: "In the presence of sages, you can see how to perfect your thoughts. In the presence of fools, you must awaken yourself."

18   The Master said: "In serving your mother and father, admonish them gently. If they understand, and yet choose not to follow your advice, deepen your reverence without losing faith. And however exhausting this may be, avoid resentment."

19   The Master said: "While your mother and father are alive, never travel to far-off places. Or if you must, always follow a definite plan."

20   The Master said: "If you leave your father's Way unchanged for all three years of mourning, you are indeed a worthy child."

21   The Master said: "Never forget your parents' age. Though it fills you with dread, it also fills you with joy."

22   The Master said: "The ancients spoke little. They were too ashamed when their actions fell short of their words."

23   The Master said: "To lose by caution is rare indeed."

24   The Master said: "This is what the noble-minded aspire to: slow to speak and quick to act."

25   The Master said: "Integrity's never alone. It always has neighbors."

26   Adept Yu said: "If you scold your sovereign too often, you'll end up disgraced. If you scold your friend too often, you'll end up alone."

月　顏　皇　追　旦　歷
寶　氏　立　且　仁　元
　　里　心　禮　閒
布　聰　念　器　君　玄
元　家　襄　樂　以
　　爲　虛　之　注　水
百　魯　世　普　同　敬
主　親　禮　待　濟
改　里　樂　鍾　異　遠
　　并　陵　齊　遲　官

v   Kung-yeh Ch'ang

1   The Master said Kung-yeh Ch'ang[1] would make a fine husband, for although he's been in prison, it was through no fault of his own. And so the Master gave his daughter in marriage to him.

The Master said Nan Jung[2] wouldn't be overlooked in a country that abides in the Way, and wouldn't be punished in a country that ignores the Way. And so the Master gave his brother's daughter in marriage to him.

2   Of Adept Chien,[3] the Master said: "Noble-minded indeed! And if there was no one noble-minded in Lu, how did he get that way?"

3   Adept Kung asked: "And what about me?"
     "You're an implement," replied the Master.
     "What kind of implement?"
     "A sacrificial vessel of jade."

4   Someone said: "Jan Yung[4] is Humane, but he's hardly eloquent."

"What good is eloquence?" said the Master. "If you badger people with clever talk, they usually just end up hating you. I don't know if he's Humane, but what good is eloquence?"

5   When the Master told him to take a position in government, Ch'i-tiao K'ai[5] replied: "I still can't trust myself that far."

The Master was delighted.

6   The Master said: "The Way's lost and forgotten in this land. If I found a raft and set out across the sea, I doubt anyone but Lu would follow me."

Hearing this, Adept Lu[6] was elated.

"Lu's much fonder of courage than I am," said the Master, "but his judgment is poor indeed."

7   Meng Wu-po asked if Adept Lu was Humane, and the Master replied: "I don't know."

When Meng asked again, the Master said: "In a nation of

a thousand war-chariots, Lu could be Minister of Defense. But I don't know if he's Humane."

"And Jan Ch'iu – what about Jan Ch'iu?"

"In a city of a thousand families or a territory ruled by a noble house of a hundred war-chariots, Ch'iu could be regent.[7] But I don't know if he's Humane."

"And Adept Hua?"

"With his sash on at court, Hua could chat with visitors and guests. But I don't know if he's Humane, either."

8   The Master said to Adept Kung: "Who do you think is better, you or Yen Hui?"

"How could I even dare look at Hui?" answered Kung. "When Hui hears one thing, he understands ten. But when I hear one thing, I only understand two."

"Nothing like him!" said the Master. "You and I are nothing like him!"

9   Tsai Yü slept in the daytime. The Master said: "You can't carve much of anything from rotted wood. And you can't whitewash a wall of dung. So why bother scolding a person like Yü?

"In dealing with people," the Master added, "I once listened to their words, and then trusted them to do what they said. Now I listen to their words, and then watch what they do carefully. It was Yü that changed me."

10   The Master said: "I've never met anyone who is truly resolute."

"What about Shen Ch'eng?"

"Ch'eng – that bundle of passions? How resolute can *he* be?"

11   Adept Kung said: "I do nothing to others that I wouldn't want done to me."

"That's something you haven't quite mastered, Kung," the Master replied.

12   Adept Kung said: "When the Master talks about civility and cultivation, you can hear what he says. But when he talks about the nature of things and the Way of Heaven, you can't hear a word."

13   When Adept Lu heard a precept, his one fear was that he might hear another before he could put the first into practice.

14   Adept Kung asked: "If he was so treacherous, why is Lord K'ung Wen called *Wen*?"[8]

"He was diligent in his love of learning," replied the Master, "and he was never ashamed to seek answers from those beneath him. That's why he's called *Wen.*"

15   The Master said Prime Minister Ch'an embodied four aspects of the noble-minded Way: humble in living his life and reverent in serving his lord, generous in nurturing the people and responsible in employing them.

16   The Master said: "Yen P'ing-chung[9] was a master of friendship. He still treated old friends with reverence."

17   The Master said: "Tsang Wen-chung[10] kept a sacred divination tortoise among mountain-carved beams and

duckweed-carved pillars, as if he were an Emperor. What kind of wisdom is that?"

18   Adept Chang said: "Tzu-wen was appointed Prime Minister three times without ever showing delight. And he resigned three times without ever showing resentment. Instead, he dutifully explained the operation of his government to his successors. What do you think of such a man?"

"He was loyal indeed," replied the Master.

"And was he Humane?"

"I don't know," replied the Master. "Would such things make him Humane?"

Adept Chang began again: "When Ts'ui Tzu killed the Ch'i sovereign, Lord Ch'en Wen was a minister who had ten teams of horses, but he abandoned everything and left. He went to another country – but soon, saying *They're just like our grand Ts'ui Tzu here,* he left. He went to the next country – and soon, saying the same thing, he left there too. What do you think of such a man?"

"He was pure indeed."

"And was he Humane?"

"I don't know," replied the Master. "Would such things make him Humane?"

19 Lord Chi Wen thought three times before taking any action. When the Master heard this, he said: "Twice is plenty enough."

20 The Master said: "People say Lord Ning Wu[11]

was a sage when his country followed the Way
and a fool when his country abandoned the Way.

We may master his wisdom, but never his foolishness."

21 When he was in Ch'en, the Master said: "Back home! Let's go back home! The young in our villages are full of impetuous ambition. They've perfected eloquence and grace, but know nothing about proper measure."

22 The Master said: "Po Yi and Shu Ch'i[12] never harbored old grudges, and so had little use for rancor."

23 The Master said: "How can people say Wei-sheng Kao was forthright? When someone came to him begging for vinegar, he borrowed some from a neighbor and gave it to them."

24   The Master said: "Clever talk, ingratiating looks, fawning reverence: Tso-ch'iu Ming found that shameful, and so do I. Friendly while harboring resentment: Tso-ch'iu Ming found that shameful, too, and so do I."

25   When Yen Hui and Adept Lu were attending him, the Master said: "Why don't you each tell me what your greatest ambition is?"

"I'd like to share horses and carriages, robes and light furs with friends," said Lu, "to see them well-used, and then rest content."

"I'd like never to promote my virtues," said Yen Hui, "and never to burden others."

Adept Lu then said: "Now Master, we'd like to hear your greatest ambition."

"To comfort the old, to trust my friends, and to cherish the young."

26   The Master said: "It's hopeless! I never see people who can recognize their own faults and then inwardly accuse themselves."

27   The Master said: "In a village of ten homes, you could certainly find someone who stands by words as faithfully as me, but no one who so loves learning."

顧氏聖，顥氏聖心念，真家元官改。

一旦追臬顧，氏聖

元仁扜立孔氏

聞玄禮心聖顥

君汙器念嬰

周以樂真家弁

雉主之盧宮元

敬水昔世魯

味涂待禮親自

真昊海建樂里弁

漫齋陵弁改

聞遲建官

VI   Jan Yung Is One Who

1   The Master said: "Jan Yung is one who could take the Emperor's seat and sit facing south."

Jan Yung asked about Tzu-sang Po-tzu, and the Master said: "Yes, with his mastery of simplicity, he too could take the Emperor's seat."

"To act simply because your life is reverent," replied Yung, "isn't that enough to lead the people? But to act simply because your life is simple, isn't that simplicity gone too far?"

"Yes. What you say is quite true."

2   Duke Ai asked which of the disciples had a true love of learning.

"Yen Hui had a true love of learning," replied Confucius. "He never blamed others and never made the same mistake twice. Unfortunately, destiny[1] allowed him but a brief life, and now he's dead. Now, I know of no one who loves learning."

3   When Adept Hua was sent to Ch'i on a mission, his mother was running short of supplies, so Jan Ch'iu asked that she be given grain.

"Give her a basketful," replied the Master.

Jan Ch'iu asked for more.

"Alright, give her a bushel," replied the Master.

Jan gave her twenty-five bushels, whereupon the Master said: "Hua set off for Ch'i riding a sleek horse and wearing light furs. I have heard that the noble-minded give to help the needy, not to subsidize the wealthy."

4   When he was appointed regent, Yüan Szu[2] was offered nine hundred measures of grain, but he refused. The Master said: "Why refuse? Aren't there people in your neighborhoods and villages who need that grain?"

5   Speaking of Jan Yung, the Master said: "If it were born of a common field ox, we may not want to use it in the earth sacrifice, though it have fine horns and sorrel hide – but would mountains and rivers reject it?"

6   The Master said: "Yen Hui can empty his mind of everything but Humanity for three months, and never falter. Others may cling to it for a day or month, but that's all."

7   Lord Chi K'ang asked: "Is Adept Lu worthy of government office?"

"Lu is resolute," replied the Master. "If you appoint him, what could go wrong?"

"And Adept Kung – is he worthy of government office?"

"Kung is wise. If you appoint him, what could go wrong?"

"What about Jan Ch'iu?"

"Ch'iu is skillful. If you appoint him, what could go wrong?"[3]

8   When the House of Chi wanted to appoint him regent in Pi, Min Tzu-ch'ien[4] said: "Find some diplomatic way of declining for me. If they come after me again, I'll have to cross the Wen River and live in Ch'i."

9   When Jan Po-niu[5] fell ill, the Master went to visit him. Standing outside the window and holding his hand, the

Master said: "He's dying! It's destiny, pure and simple. But how could such a man have such a disease? How could such a man have such a disease?"

10   The Master said: "How noble Yen Hui is! To live in a meager lane with nothing but some rice in a split-bamboo bowl and some water in a gourd cup – no one else could bear such misery. But it doesn't even bother Hui. His joy never wavers. O, how noble Hui is!"

11   Jan Ch'iu said: "It isn't that I'm not happy with your Way, Master, but I'm just not strong enough."

"If someone isn't strong enough," replied the Master, "they give up along the Way. But you'd already set your limits in advance."

12   Speaking to Adept Hsia, the Master said: "Be a noble-minded scholar, not a small-minded one."

13   When Adept Yu was regent in Wu Ch'eng, the Master asked: "Have you come across anyone surprising?"

"There's a certain T'an-t'ai Mieh-ming," replied Yu. "He never takes shortcuts, and he's never come to my office except on official business."

14   The Master said: "Meng Chih-fan[6] never boasts. When the army fled, he brought up the rear. Then when he was coming in through the gates, he spurred his horse on, saying *It wasn't courage that kept me behind. This horse just won't go any faster.*"

15   The Master said: "These days, without Priest T'o's slick tongue and Chao's good looks, you'll never get away unscathed."

16   The Master said: "Who can set out without using a door? How is it, then, no one uses this Way?"

17   The Master said: "People are too wild when nature dominates culture in them, and too tame when culture dominates nature. But when nature and culture are blended and balanced in them, they're noble-minded."

18   The Master said: "Honesty is our very life. Without it, to elude death is sheer luck."

19   The Master said: "To understand something is nothing like loving it. And to love something is nothing like delighting in it."

20   The Master said: "You can speak of lofty things with those who've made something lofty of themselves, but not with those who haven't."

21   Fan Ch'ih asked about wisdom, and the Master said: "Devotion to perfecting your Duties toward the people, and reverence for gods and spirits while keeping your distance from them – that can be called wisdom."

And when Fan Ch'ih asked about Humanity, the Master said: "The Humane master the difficult parts before expecting any rewards – that can be called Humanity."

22   The Master said: "The wise delight in rivers, and the Humane delight in mountains: the wise are in motion,

and the Humane still; the wise are joyful, and the Humane long-lived."

23   The Master said: "A twinkling of change could bring Ch'i to the level of Lu. And a twinkling of change could bring Lu to the Way."

24   The Master said: "A cup not a cup: A cup indeed! A cup indeed!"

25   Tsai Yü asked: "Hearing that Humanity's down in a well, wouldn't a Humane person jump in after it?"

"What makes you think that?" replied the Master. "The noble-minded can perish, but they can't be entrapped. They can be deceived, but they can't be snared in nets."

26   The Master said: "The noble-minded are well-versed in culture and well-grounded in Ritual, so how could they ever go wrong?"

27   The Master went to visit Lady Nan.[7] When he saw how displeased Adept Lu was, the Master declared: "Heaven will renounce me if I've done anything wrong. Heaven will indeed renounce me."

28   The Master said: "The constant commonplace[8] radiates such Integrity – it's boundless! And yet, it's been rare among the people for a very long time."

29   Adept Kung said: "How would you describe a person who sows all the people with blessings and assists everyone in the land? Could such a person be called Humane?"

"What does this have to do with Humanity?" replied the Master. "If you must have a name, call this person a *sage*. For even the enlightened Emperors Yao[9] and Shun would seem lacking by comparison. As for Humanity: if you want to make a stand, help others make a stand, and if you want to reach your goal, help others reach their goal. Consider yourself and treat others accordingly: this is the method of Humanity."

肩　頋　鼻　延　旦　士
　　氏　于　立　抒　仁
聖　心　禮　玄　聞
希　家　念　器　汙　君
元　宮　其　樂　以　屏
　　魯　廬　之　汪　獲
　　世　普　昔　水　敬
百　親　禮　待　浹　咏
主　里　樂　鍾　海　思
　　并　陵　　　橋
　　宮　遲

VII   Transmitting Insight, But

1   The Master said: "Transmitting insight, but never creating insight, standing by my words and devoted to the ancients: perhaps I'm a little like that old sage, P'eng."[1]

2   The Master said: "To understand through dark silence, to study without tiring, to teach without faltering: how could such things still be difficult for me?"

3   The Master said: "These are the kinds of things I find troubling:

> *possessing Integrity without cultivating it*
> *and possessing knowledge without deepening it,*
>
> *knowing Duties without following them*
> *and knowing failings without changing them."*

4   At leisure, the Master was loose and breezy.

5 The Master said: "I've gotten so feeble! It's been forever since I dreamed of the sage Duke Chou."[2]

6 The Master said: "Devote yourself to the Way, depend on Integrity, rely on Humanity, and wander in the arts."

7 The Master said: "I never refuse to teach anyone, not even those so lowly they come offering nothing but a few strips of dried meat."

8 The Master said: "I never instruct those who aren't full of passion, and I never enlighten those who aren't struggling to explain themselves.

"If I show you one corner and you can't show me the other three, I'll say nothing more."

9 If he was seated next to someone in mourning, the Master never ate his fill.

10   If he'd already wept that day, the Master wouldn't sing.

11   Speaking to Yen Hui, the Master said:

> *"A leader when appointed to office*
> *and a recluse when sent away.*

Only you and I have perfected this."

"If you were leading the Three Armies," asked Adept Lu, "who would you take with you?"

"A man who attacks tigers unarmed and crosses rivers without boats, willing to die without the least regret – that's a man I'd never take with me. The man I'd take always approaches difficulties with due caution and always succeeds by planning carefully."

12   The Master said: "If there were an honorable way to get rich, I'd do it, even if it meant being a stooge standing around with a whip. But there isn't an honorable way, so I just do what I like."

13   The Master treated three things with the greatest care: fasting, war, and sickness.

14   In Ch'i, after hearing the music of Emperor Shun, it was three months before the Master noticed the taste of food again. He just kept saying, "I never dreamed music was capable of such things."

15   Jan Ch'iu said: "Does our Master support the Wei ruler?"[3]

"Yes, I should ask him about that," replied Adept Kung.

So Kung went in to see the Master and asked: "Who were Po Yi and Shu Ch'i?"

"Wise men of ancient times," replied Confucius.

"Did they harbor any resentments?"

"They devoted themselves to Humanity, and so became Humane. How could they harbor any resentments?"

Kung returned to Jan Ch'iu and said: "No, the Master doesn't support him."

16   The Master said: "Poor food and water for dinner, a bent arm for a pillow – that is where joy resides. For me, wealth and renown without honor are nothing but drifting clouds."

17   The Master said: "Grant me a few more years. After studying Change[4] for fifty years, I'll surely be free of serious flaws."

18   The Master never used Lu dialect[5] for *The Book of Songs, The Book of History*, or the observance of Ritual. Never.

19   When Duke She[6] asked Adept Lu about Confucius, Lu ignored him.

Later, the Master said: "Why didn't you just say something like this: *He's a man so full of passion that he forgets to eat, and so full of joy that he forgets to worry. He's never even noticed old age coming over him.*"

20   The Master said: "I am not one who was born with great wisdom. I love the ancients and diligently seek wisdom among them."

21   The Master never spoke of the supernatural, violence, disorder, or gods and spirits.

22   The Master said: "Out walking with two companions, I'm sure to be in my teacher's company. The good in one I adopt in myself; the evil in the other I change in myself."

23   The Master said: "My Integrity is born of Heaven. So what can Huan T'ui's[7] assassins do to me?"

24   The Master said: "My students, do you think I'm being secretive? But I'm hiding nothing from you. I share my entire life with you, my friends. And that is who I am."

25   The Master taught four things: culture, conduct, loyalty, and standing by your words.

26   The Master said: "I have no hope of meeting a true sage. To meet someone noble-minded would be enough."

The Master said: "I have no hope of meeting a truly virtuous and benevolent person. To meet someone who's mastered constancy would be enough. But constancy is impossible if you imagine yourself having when you have not, full when you're empty, prosperous when you're destitute."

27   The Master fished with hooks, not nets, and he never shot roosting birds.

28   The Master said: "I suppose there are some who don't need wisdom to live wisely. I am not so lucky. I've heard countless things, choosing what is good and adopting it in myself. I've seen countless things and remembered them well. This is a lesser form of wisdom."

29　　The people of Hu Village had no interest in the teachings of Confucius. A young boy came to see the Master. When the Master saw that his disciples were perplexed, he said: "Accepting this boy's visit does not mean accepting his entire life. Why be so demanding? If someone purifies himself to come here, we can accept that purification without accepting his entire past."

30　　The Master said: "Is Humanity really so far away? We need only want it, and here it is!"

31　　The Minister of Justice in Ch'en asked whether Duke Chao of Lu understood Ritual.

"Yes, he does," replied Confucius.

After Confucius left, the minister bowed to Wu-ma Ch'i,[8] inviting him to approach, and said: "I have heard that the noble-minded show no partiality, and yet it seems that some are very partial indeed. The woman Chao married is from the royal house of Wu, and so belongs to his own clan. He just renamed her Lady Wu Meng. If he understands Ritual, who doesn't?"

When Wu-ma Ch'i told him about this, the Master said: "How lucky I am. If I make a mistake, someone is sure to recognize it."

32   When someone sang a song that he liked, the Master always asked them to sing it again before he joined in.

33   The Master said: "No one has been so devoted to learning and culture. But when it comes to the practices of a noble-minded life, I haven't done so well."

34   The Master said: "That I've become a sage and mastered Humanity? How could I say that of myself? I work at it and teach it, never tiring. You could say that much. But no more."

"And that's exactly what we students have failed to learn," said Adept Hua.

35   The Master was terribly sick. Adept Lu asked if he might offer a prayer, and the Master said: "Is there such prayer?"

"There is," replied Lu. *The Book of Eulogies says: We pray for you to the gods and spirits above and below.*

"My life has been my prayer," responded the Master.

36   The Master said: "The extravagant are soon pompous, and the frugal soon resolute. Better resolute than pompous."

37   The Master said: "The noble-minded are calm and steady. Little people are forever fussing and fretting."

38   The Master was genial and yet austere, awesome and yet not fierce, reverent and yet content.

顥月
氏　聖賢
　　賜
　家東元
居魯
　魯親百
　禮里主
陵并不
官　改官

樂　立玄禮
心念　真世禮樂陵迟

延立禮器樂　音待鍾磬

具拚　汙以往水添法

土仁聞君同權敬哦思隱

VIII Surely T'ai Po

1   The Master said: "Surely T'ai Po[1] can be called a master of Integrity. Three times he declined to rule all beneath Heaven, and he did it so discreetly the people never praised him."

2   The Master said: "Reverence becomes tedium without Ritual, and caution becomes timidity. Without Ritual, courage becomes recklessness, and truth becomes intolerance.

"When noble-minded leaders honor their parents, the people feel called to Humanity. And when leaders never forget old friends, the people live open and true."

3   Master Tseng was terribly sick. He summoned his disciples and said: "Look at my feet. Look at my hands. The *Songs* say:

Trembling in watchful terror –
as if facing a deep abyss,
as if walking over thin ice.[2]

Whatever happens, I know now that I am free, my little ones."

4   $\mathcal{M}$aster Tseng was terribly sick. When Lord Meng Ching came to ask how he was doing, he said:

> *"When birds are about to die,*
> *their cries are full of sorrow.*
>
> *When humans are about to die,*
> *their words are full of virtue.*

In following the Way, the noble-minded treasure three things: a manner free of violence and arrogance, a countenance full of sincerity and trust, a voice free of vulgarity and impropriety.

"As for sacrificial vessels, that is the business of appointed officers."

5   $\mathcal{M}$aster Tseng said: "To be capable, and yet seek advice from the incapable; to be richly endowed, and yet

seek advice from the poorly endowed; having as if having not; full as if empty; offended, but never accusing. I had a friend long ago who lived that way."[3]

6   Master Tseng said: "A man who can be entrusted with a small orphan or a large state, who faces a great crisis and remains unshaken – is he not noble-minded? He is indeed noble-minded!"

7   Master Tseng said: "You must be resolute and broad-minded, for the burden is heavy and the Way long. When Humanity is your burden, is it not indeed heavy? And when the Way ends only at death, is it not indeed long?"

8   The Master said: "Be incited by the *Songs*, established by Ritual, and perfected by music."

9   The Master said: "You can make the people follow the Way, but you can't make them understand it."

10   The Master said: "If courageous people suffer from poverty, they'll soon tear the country apart. Unless they've mastered Humanity, anyone whose sufferings are great would tear it apart with abandon."

11   The Master said: "A person may be as nobly endowed as Duke Chou, but all that isn't enough to inspire admiration if they aren't humble and generous."

12   The Master said: "A person who can study for three years and never worry about a salary – that is very difficult to find."

13   The Master said: "Love learning and trust it deeply. Guard the Way of virtue and benevolence unto death. Never enter a dangerous country, and never inhabit a country in turmoil.

"When all beneath Heaven abides in the Way, make yourself known; and when the Way's lost, stay hidden. When the Way rules in your country, there's shame in poverty and obscurity; and when the Way's lost in your country, there's shame in wealth and renown."

14 The Master said: "Unless you've been appointed to office, don't fuss and fret over the business of government."

15 The Master said: "When Music-master Chih begins the climax of 'Ospreys Calling,'[4] what a swelling sea of sound fills the ears!"

16 The Master said: "Wild and yet dishonest, base and yet insincere, simple-hearted and yet untrustworthy – I'll never understand such people."

17 The Master said: "Study as if you'll never know enough, as if you're afraid of losing it all."

18 The Master said: "How majestic, how exalted and majestic Shun and Yü[5] were: all beneath Heaven was theirs, and yet it was nothing to them!"

19   The Master said: "Great indeed was the rule of Emperor Yao! Heaven alone is truly majestic, exalted and majestic, and only Yao could equal it. He was boundless, so vast and boundless the people couldn't even name him.

"How exalted and majestic his achievements! How bright and glorious the ways of culture he created."[6]

20   Shun had five ministers, and all beneath Heaven was well governed. And Emperor Wu, sage founder of the Chou, once said: "I have ten fine ministers."

Therefore, Confucius said: *"Talent is rare,* as the saying goes, and isn't it true? The time of Yao and Shun was rich in talent. And since one was his mother, Wu really only had nine ministers. Of all beneath Heaven, the Chou held two parts in three, and yet still served the Shang house humbly. Its Integrity was absolute."

21   The Master said: "To me, Yü seems beyond all criticism. He ate the simplest food, but made sumptuous offerings to ancestral gods and spirits. He wore the plainest robes, but wore exquisite regalia for sacrifice and ceremony.

He lived in the humblest house, but devoted his energy to irrigation channels and canals. To me, Yü seems beyond all criticism."

CHAPTER VIII

顧氏聖　　家元魯親里弄官

臬立心念　真廬世禮樂陵

廷禮器業　　普待鍾

旦將玄汙以佳水齊

仁聞君辰權敬

IX The Master Rarely

1   The Master rarely spoke of profit or destiny or Humanity.

2   A villager in Ta Hsiang said: "Great indeed is Confucius! His erudition is truly vast – and still, he's lived without fame and renown."

When the Master heard this, he said to his disciples: "What shall I be – a charioteer or an archer? I'll be a charioteer!"

3   The Master said: "Ritual calls for caps of linen, but now everyone uses black silk. It's more frugal, so I follow the common practice.

"Ritual calls for bowing before ascending the stairs, but now everyone bows only at the top of the stairs. That's too presumptuous, so even though it violates the common practice, I bow before ascending."

4   The Master had freed himself of four things: idle speculation, certainty, inflexibility, and conceit.

5   When he was ambushed in K'uang, the Master said: "Emperor Wen[1] is long since dead, but doesn't culture [wen] still live here in me? If Heaven wanted this culture to end, it wouldn't survive such deaths. But Heaven's let this culture continue, so what can these K'uang people do to me?"

6   Speaking to Adept Kung, a grand minister asked: "Your master is a great sage, isn't he? And yet, he's learned so many useful skills!"

"It's true Heaven meant him to be a sage," Kung replied, "but he learned many useful skills, too."

When the Master heard this, he said: "That grand minister knows me well! We were humble and poor when I was young: that's why I can do so many practical things. But do the noble-minded need all these skills? No, not so many as this."

7   According to Lao, the Master said: "I was never appointed to office: that's why I'm so handy."

8   The Master said: "Am I a man of great wisdom? Hardly! Even when a simple person brings me a question, my mind goes utterly blank. I just thrash it out until I've exhausted every possibility."

9   The Master said: "The Phoenix hasn't come and the river hasn't revealed its divine chart.[2] This is the end of me."

10   Whenever he met someone in mourning, someone in ceremonial robes, or someone blind – the Master would stand or humbly step aside.

11   Sighing heavily, Yen Hui said: "The more I gaze up into it, the higher it gets, and the more I bore down into it, the harder it gets. In reverence, I see it before me, and suddenly it's behind me.

"The Master is good at luring people on, step by step. He

uses culture to broaden us, and Ritual to secure us. Though I often feel like quitting, I can't, because whenever it seems I've reached my limit, something seems to rise before me, lofty and majestic. But however much I long to go there, the path remains a mystery."

12   The Master was terribly sick, so Adept Lu had the disciples dress up as the kind of retainers he had as a minister. The sickness let up for a time, and the Master said to them: "Lu's always been conjuring these deceits. If I pretend to have retainers when I have none, who am I deceiving? Am I deceiving Heaven?

"Don't you think I'd rather face death in your arms than in the arms of strange clerks? I may not have a grand funeral, but I'm hardly dying in some roadside ditch."

13   Adept Kung said: "If I have a beautiful piece of jade, what should I do – lock it away in a case or look for the best price and sell it?"

"Sell it!" was the Master's answer. "Sell it! I'm just waiting to get the right offer for mine!"

14   The Master wanted to go live among the nine wild tribes in the east.

Someone asked: "How could you bear such vulgarity?"

"If someone noble-minded lived there," replied the Master, "how could vulgarity be a problem?"

15   The Master said: "After returning from Wei to Lu, I trued up music and returned the *Songs* to its original form."

16   The Master said: *"Serve family elders when home, serve ruling officials when away, leave nothing undone when mourning, never drink yourself into a stupor* – how could such things still be difficult for me?"

17   Standing beside a river, the Master said: "Everything passes away like this, day and night, never resting."

18   The Master said: "I've never seen anyone for whom loving Integrity is like loving a beautiful woman."

19 The Master said: "It's like building a mountain: even if I don't stop until I'm only short one last basket of dirt – still, I've stopped. It's like leveling ground: even if I'm just starting out with the first basketful – still, I'm forging ahead."

20 The Master said: "If there's anyone who was never careless about what I said, it was Yen Hui."

21 Speaking of Yen Hui, the Master said: "How sad – to watch him forge ahead so resolutely, and never see how far he could go."[3]

22 The Master said: "There are, indeed, sprouts that never come to flower. And there are flowers that never bear fruit."

23 The Master said: "Hold the young in awe. How can we know their generation will not equal our own? Only when they've lived to be forty or fifty without any distinction – only then are they no longer worthy of our awe."

24 The Master said: "Worthy admonitions cannot fail to inspire us, but what matters is changing ourselves. Reverent advice cannot fail to encourage us, but what matters is acting on it. Encouraged without acting, inspired without changing – there's nothing to be done for such people."

25 The Master said: "Above all, be loyal and stand by your words. Befriend only those who are kindred spirits. And when you're wrong, don't be afraid to change."

26 The Master said: "Vast armies can be robbed of their commander, but even the simplest people cannot be robbed of their free will."

27 The Master said: "To wear threadbare hemp robes and stand without shame among those wearing lavish furs of fox and badger – isn't that what Adept Lu is like?

He hates nothing and covets nothing.
How could he be anything but good?"[4]

Adept Lu began chanting these lines to himself over and over. Finally, the Master said: "That isn't enough to make someone all that good, is it?"

CHAPTER IX

28　　The Master said: "Only after the seasons turn cold can we truly know the resolve of pine and cypress."

29　　The Master said: "The wise never doubt. The Humane never worry. The brave never fear."

30　　The Master said: "Some can study with you, but not follow the Way with you. Some can follow the Way with you, but not stand firm with you in its principles. And some can stand firm with you in its principles, but not join you in putting them into practice."

31　　Lavish aspen-plum blossoms
　　　tremble and sway alone:

　　　I haven't stopped loving you,
　　　but your home is so far away.[5]

The Master said: "If he'd really loved her, he wouldn't have worried about the distance."

頊氏聖嬰弟元百主改官

立心念家魯親里弁宮遲

延禮器津世禮樂陵理

持玄汙以注水濟海鍾

是仁聞君同權敬

歷

1   In his native village, Confucius was simple and sincere, as if he couldn't speak. But at court or ancestral temple, though always cautious and reverent, he spoke openly and easily.

At court, speaking with lower officials, he was forthright. Speaking with high officials, he was diplomatic. And speaking with the sovereign, he was wary – wary and self-assured.

2   When his sovereign summoned him to receive a guest, his demeanor suddenly changed and his steps grew reverent. When he bowed to his waiting colleagues, his right arm reached out, then his left, but his robes hung straight and true. Then he'd hurry forward, sleeves speading like noble wings. And once the guest had departed, he promptly returned to report: "The guest is no longer looking back."

3   Entering the palace gates, he closed in on himself, as if the gates weren't big enough. Stopping, he never

stood in the middle of the gate, and passing through, he never stepped on the threshold.

Passing the royal platform, his demeanor suddenly changed, his steps grew reverent, and words seemed to fail him.

Raising his robe on ascending to the hall, he closed in on himself, focusing his *ch'i*[1] until he scarcely seemed to breathe. And leaving, his expression relaxing on descending the first step, he seemed happy and content. At the bottom of the steps, he'd hurry forward as if borne on noble wings. And then, returning to his station, he grew wary again.

4   Carrying his official scepter, he closed in on himself, as if it were too heavy. He held the top as if bowing, and the bottom as if making an offering. His demeanor turned solemn, and he walked attentively, as if his steps were preordained.

In making Ritual offerings, he looked tranquil. And alone with his sovereign, he was at ease and cheerful.

5   Such a noble-minded man never wore purple or maroon trim. And in his informal robes, he never wore red or chestnut brown.

In summer heat, he chose thin open-weave robes, worn over something light to set them off.

With black silk, he wore lambskin furs. With undyed silk, he wore deerskin furs. And with yellow silk, he wore fox furs.

His informal furs were long, with the right sleeve cut short so his hand was free. And for sleeping, he always wore robes half as long as he himself was.

Because fox and badger furs are so thick, he wore them at home.

Unless in mourning, he wore all his waist-jewels.

Other than ceremonial skirts, his robes were all sewn pieces.

When offering condolences, he never wore lavish lambskin furs or caps of black silk. For the new moon, he went to court in his full court regalia. And during purification for the sacrifice, he wore bright robes of plain linen.

6   During purification for the sacrifice, he changed what he ate and where he sat. Polished rice was fine, and minced meat. He didn't eat sour rice or rancid fish or spoiled meat. He didn't eat anything that looked or smelled bad. He didn't eat food that wasn't well-cooked and in season, or food that wasn't properly sliced and served with the proper

sauce. Even when there was plenty of meat, he only ate enough to balance the *ch'i* of rice. Only in wine did he set no limits, but he never drank himself into confusion. He wouldn't drink wine from a wineshop or eat meat from a market. And though he didn't refuse ginger, he ate it only sparingly.

After the state sacrifice, he never kept the meat overnight. And he never kept meat more than three days after the family sacrifice. After three days, he wouldn't eat it.

He didn't speak at meals, and he didn't talk in bed.

He made an offering of even the simplest rice and vegetable, broth and melon – and he did so with the greatest solemnity.

7   If the mat wasn't laid straight, he wouldn't sit.

When the people of his village were drinking wine, he left only after the elders with walking-sticks had left.

8   When the villagers were out driving evil spirits away, he put on his court robes and stood like a host on the eastern steps.

9   When sending his regards to someone in another country, he bowed twice as the messenger set out.

10   When Lord Chi K'ang sent a certain medicine to him as a gift, Confucius bowed twice, then accepted it, saying: "I'm not familiar with this, so I dare not try it."

11   One day the stables burned down. When he returned from court, the Master asked: "Was anyone hurt?" He didn't ask about the horses.

12   When the sovereign sent a gift of food, he straightened his mat and dined immediately. When the sovereign sent a gift of uncooked food, he cooked it and made an offering. When the sovereign sent a gift of live animals, he always raised them.

When serving at the royal table, he always began with rice once the sovereign had made offerings.

13   When he was sick and his sovereign came to visit, he laid facing east with his court robes draped over him and his sash trailed out across the bed.

14   When summoned by his sovereign, he set out at once, without even waiting for his horses to be harnessed.

15   When he was in the Grand Temple, the Master asked questions about everything he saw.

16   When a friend died and there was no home to which the body could be sent, he said: "Let the funeral be in my home."

17   A friend might send a gift, even something so lavish as a horse and carriage, but he never bowed unless it was sacrificial meat.

18   In bed, he never lay facing north like a corpse. At home, he moved without formality.

19   Whenever he met someone in mourning garments, even if it was someone he knew well, his expression turned solemn. If his robes were sometimes informal when

he met those who were blind or wearing ceremonial caps, his demeanor was always appropriate. For those in mourning and those carrying official documents, he bowed down to the crossbars of his carriage.

When a lavish feast was served, his expression changed and he rose to his feet in reverence for the host.

Startled by a sudden thunderclap or violent wind, his expression always turned solemn.

20 When mounting the carriage, he stood square and gripped the mounting-cord. And while riding in the carriage, he always looked outside but never shouted or pointed.

21 Seeing such an expression, it startled away. It drifted and soared, then settled down again.

He said:

> "A pheasant on the mountain bridge:
> Such omens! Such omens it brings!"

When Adept Lu presented offerings, it sniffed three times and set off.

顏氏聖□和元

有氏聖雙家宮魯親里并官

興立心念真應世禮樂陵遲

追抒禮器梁之普祷鍾□理

直□玄浮以注水沇浩迁□

士仁聞君居權敬祀思□聞

XI Studies Begin

1   The Master said: *"Those whose studies begin with Ritual and music are commoners. Those whose studies end with Ritual and music are noble-minded.*

"If I employed such a saying, I'd say studies begin there."

2   The Master said: "Of my followers in Ch'en and Ts'ai, not one came far enough to enter my gate."

3   For Integrity: Yen Hui, Min Tzu-ch'ien, Jan Po-niu, and Jan Yung.

For eloquence: Tsai Yü and Adept Kung.

For governing: Jan Ch'iu and Adept Lu.

For cultivation: Adept Yu and Adept Hsia.

4   The Master said: "Yen Hui's never helped me much: no matter what I say, he's delighted."

5   The Master said: "What a marvelous child Min Tzu-ch'ien is! In all his family says about him, there isn't a flaw to be found."

6   Nan Jung chanted the lines about a white-jade scepter[1] over and over to himself. Confucius married his brother's daughter to him.

7   Lord Chi K'ang asked which of the disciples had a true love of learning.

"There was a certain Yen Hui who had a true love of learning," replied Confucius. "Unfortunately, destiny allowed him but a brief life, and now he's dead. Now there's no one like him."

8   When Yen Hui died, his father wanted the Master to sell his carriage so they could buy an outer coffin for his son.

The Master said: "Whether they are gifted or not, we all praise our own children. When my son, Po-yü, died, he had a coffin but no outer coffin. I couldn't sell my carriage so he could have an outer coffin. I was in attendance on high ministers: to go on foot would have been improper."

9   **W**hen Yen Hui died, the Master cried: "O, Heaven's killing me! It's killing me!"

10   **W**hen Yen Hui died, the Master's mourning was extravagant.

"You're being awfully extravagant," said his followers.

"Am I?" replied the Master. "If this man's death doesn't call forth extravagant mourning, whose will?"

11   **W**hen Yen Hui died, the disciples wanted to give him a lavish burial. But the Master said: "No, you can't do that."

The disciples went ahead and gave him a lavish burial anyway. Afterward, the Master said to them: "Hui treated me like a father. And now I've failed to treat him like a son. But it wasn't my doing: it was yours."

12   When Adept Lu asked about serving ghosts and spirits, the Master said: "You haven't learned to serve the living, so how could you serve ghosts?"

"Might I ask about death?"

"You don't understand life," the Master replied, "so how could you understand death?"

13   In attendance on the Master – Min Tzu-ch'ien was diplomatic, Adept Lu was dynamic, Jan Ch'iu and Adept Kung were forthright. The Master was pleased. But he said: "People like Adept Lu never live to die of old age."

14   When the officers of Lu were planning to rebuild the treasury building, Min Tzu-ch'ien said: "Just rebuild the old one. Why make it new and different?"

"He's a man who rarely speaks," commented the Master, "but when he does speak, he's always right on target."

15   The Master said: "What is Lu doing, playing his *se*^{2} here inside my gate?"

At this, the disciples' reverence for Lu began to fade. But

the Master said: "He may not have entered my grand hall, but Adept Lu has indeed ascended the stairs."

16   When Adept Kung asked who was most worthy, Adept Chang or Adept Hsia, the Master said: "Chang always goes too far, and Hsia always stops short."

"Then hasn't Chang surpassed Hsia?" asked Kung.

"Going too far isn't much different from stopping short," replied the Master.

17   The Chi family patriarch had grown wealthier than Duke Chou himself, and still Jan Ch'iu kept gathering taxes for him, adding greatly to his wealth.

The Master said: "He's no follower of mine. If you sounded the drums and attacked him, my little ones, it wouldn't be such a bad thing."

18   Adept Kao[3] is stupid, and Master Tseng dull. Adept Chang is eccentric, and Adept Lu crude.

19   The Master said: "Yen Hui's nearly made it: He's almost always empty.

"Adept Kung, on the other hand, refused his destiny. He went into business instead and grew rich, for his speculations are almost always right on target."

20   When Adept Chang asked about the Way people of virtue and benevolence follow, the Master said: "They never follow in the footsteps of others, and they never enter the inner chambers."

21   The Master said: "Someone's words may be true and sincere – but does that mean they're noble-minded or just full of pretense?"

22   When Adept Lu asked if he should hurry to put sage advice into practice, the Master said: "Your father and elder brother are still alive, so how can you hurry to put sage advice into practice?"

When Jan Ch'iu asked if he should hurry to put sage advice into practice, the Master said: "Of course you should hurry to put sage advice into practice."

At this, Adept Hua said: "When Lu asked if he should hurry to put sage advice into practice, you said *Your father and elder brother are still alive.* But when Ch'iu asked if he should hurry to put sage advice into practice, you said *Of course you should hurry to put sage advice into practice.* I'm confused. Could you please explain this for me?"

"Ch'iu holds back," replied the Master, "so I urge him on. Lu has enough drive for two people, so I hold him back."

23   When the Master was ambushed in K'uang, Yen Hui fell behind.

"I thought you'd been killed!" exclaimed the Master.

"With you still alive, I wouldn't dare get myself killed."

24   Chi Tzu-jan[4] asked if Adept Lu and Jan Ch'iu could be called great ministers, and the Master said: "I would have asked about some amazing disciple, but here you've just asked about Lu and Ch'iu. What I call a great minister is one who employs the Way in serving his sovereign. If he cannot do that, he resigns. Lu and Ch'iu, on the other hand, could be called makeshift ministers."

"So they just follow any order they're given?" asked Chi Tzu-jan.

"No, not any order," replied the Master. "They'd certainly refuse to kill their fathers or their sovereigns."

25   When Adept Lu arranged to have Adept Kao appointed regent in Pi, the House of Chi's capital, the Master said: "You're ruining someone's son."[5]

"The people are there in Pi," replied Lu, "and the gods of grain. Why must erudition come from books?"

"I can't bear such clever talk," muttered the Master.

26   Adept Lu, Tseng Hsi, Jan Ch'iu, and Adept Hua were all seated in attendance. The Master said: "You think of me as being a little older than you, but I'd like to forget about respect for now. You're always saying *No one recognizes our talents.* Now, tell me openly: if someone did recognize your talents, what would you do?"

Adept Lu took the lead and said: "In a nation of a thousand war-chariots hemmed in by powerful neighbors, besieged by invading armies, famine and drought – I could bring courage and direction to the people within three years."

The Master smiled gently.

"What would you do?" he asked Ch'iu.

"In a region of only sixty to seventy square miles, or even fifty to sixty square miles – I could bring satisfaction to the people within three years. As for Ritual and music, I would leave that for someone noble-minded."

"And you?" he asked Hua.

"I don't claim any great ability in such things, but I'm anxious to learn. Then, in court gatherings and ceremonies at the ancestral temple, I might wear the caps and robes of a minor official."

"And what about you?" he asked Hsi.

As the music of his *se* faded away, Tseng Hsi[6] struck a final chord. Then he put the instrument aside, stood, and said: "My aims are quite different from those of my three colleagues."

"What harm is there in that?" asked the Master. "We each have our own ambitions."

"In late spring, when the spring clothes are made, I'd like to go wandering with a few friends and servant boys, bathe in the Yi River, enjoy the wind at Rain-Dance Altar, and then wander back home in song."

The Master sighed deeply, and said: "I'm with Hsi."

When the other three disciples left, Tseng Hsi stayed behind and asked: "What did you think of what the other three said?"

"They each have their own ambitions, that's for sure," replied the Master.

"Why did you smile at Lu?"

"A country is ruled through Ritual," replied the Master, "but there was no deference in his words. That's why I smiled."

"And Ch'iu? He wasn't asking for a country, was he?"

"How could he call a region of sixty to seventy square miles or fifty to sixty square miles anything but a country?"

"And Hua? Surely he wasn't asking for a country, was he?"

"Temple ceremonies and court gatherings – if such things aren't imperial affairs, what is? And if someone like Hua plays only a minor role, who could play a major one?"

士　旦　迺　興　顯　角
仁　抒　立　子　氏
聞　玄　禮　人　聖　寶
君　汙　器　念　嬰
同　以　築　真　家　帝
權　主　走　屋　居　元
敬　水　普　世　魯
雀　濟　待　禮　親　百
思　海　鍾　樂　里　主
　　陵　　　陵　弄　沐
　　遲　　　官　改

XII   Yen Hui

1   Yen Hui asked about Humanity, and the Master said: "Giving yourself over to Ritual – that is Humanity. If a ruler gave himself to Ritual for even a single day, all beneath Heaven would return to Humanity. For doesn't the practice of Humanity find its source first in the self, and only then in others?"

"Could you explain how giving yourself to Ritual works?" asked Yen Hui.

"Never look without Ritual. Never listen without Ritual. Never speak without Ritual. Never move without Ritual."

"I'm not terribly clever," said Yen Hui, "but I'll try to serve these words."

2   Jan Yung asked about Humanity, and the Master said: "Go out into the world as if greeting a magnificent guest. Use the people as if offering a magnificent sacrifice. And never impose on others what you would not choose for yourself. Then, there will be no resentment among the people or the great families."

"I'm not terribly clever," said Jan Yung, "but I'll try to serve these words."

3   Szu-ma Niu[1] asked about Humanity, and the Master said: "The Humane speak with slow deliberation."

"So, those who speak with slow deliberation can be called Humane?"

"It's so difficult to put words into action," replied the Master. "How can anyone fail to speak with slow deliberation?"

4   Szu-ma Niu asked about the noble-minded, and the Master said: "The noble-minded live free of sorrow and fear."

"So, those who live free of sorrow and fear can be called noble-minded?"

"When you can look within and find no taint," replied the Master, "how can anything bring you sorrow or fear?"

5   A sorrowful Szu-ma Niu said: "People all have brothers. I alone have none."

"I have heard," said Adept Hsia, "that life and death are matters of destiny, that wealth and renown are matters of

Heaven. If the noble-minded are reverent and leave nothing amiss, if they are humble toward others and observe Ritual – then all within the four seas will be their brothers. So how can you grieve over having no brothers?"

6   Adept Chang asked about discrimination, and the Master said: "To hear slander and deception and hollow accusation without acting on them, that is discrimination indeed. To hear slander and deception and hollow accusation without acting on them, that is far-sighted indeed."

7   Adept Kung asked about governing, and the Master said: "Plenty of food, plenty of weapons, and the trust of the people."

"If you couldn't have all three," asked Kung, "which would you give up first?"

"I'd give up weapons."

"And if you couldn't have both the others, which would you give up first?"

"I'd give up food," replied the Master. "There's always been death. But without trust, the people are lost."

8   Chi Tzu-ch'eng said: "A person is noble-minded by nature. How could culture make someone noble-minded?"

"To say so is a great pity," replied Adept Kung. "For once the tongue sets out, even a team of horses cannot catch it.

"Culture looks just like nature, and nature like culture. Without fur, the hide of a tiger or leopard looks just like the hide of a dog or sheep."

9   Duke Ai asked Master Yu: "It's a famine year. I don't have enough to run my government. What shall I do?"

"Why not tax people the usual one part in nine?"[2] replied Yu.

"I'm already getting two parts in nine, and I still don't have enough. How could I manage on only one part in nine?"

"When everyone has enough," said Yu, "how could you alone be in need? And when everyone's in need, how could you alone have enough?"

10   Adept Chang asked about *exalting Integrity* and *unraveling delusion*.

The Master said: "Be loyal and stand by your words.

Devote yourself to that, above all, and dwell wherever Duty rules – that's exalting Integrity.

"When you love a thing, you wish it life. When you hate a thing, you wish it death. To wish both life and death for a thing – that is delusion.

> *Maybe it's for her money,*
> *and maybe for the novelty.*"[3]

11   Duke Ching[4] asked Confucius about governing, and Confucius said: "Ruler a ruler, minister a minister, father a father, son a son."

"How splendid!" exclaimed the Duke. "Truly, if the ruler isn't a ruler, the minister a minister, the father a father, and the son a son – then even if we had grain, how could we survive to eat it?"

12   The Master said: "Someone who can settle a legal dispute having heard only one side of the story? That's Adept Lu."

Adept Lu never slept with a promise left unfulfilled.

13   The Master said: "I can hear a court case as well as anyone. But we need to make a world where there's no reason for a court case."

14   Adept Chang asked about governing, and the Master said: "Contemplate an issue tirelessly at home, then act on it loyally."

15   The Master said: "Well-versed in culture and well-grounded in Ritual – how could you ever go wrong?"

16   The Master said: "The noble-minded encourage what is beautiful in people and discourage what is ugly in them. Little people do just the opposite."

17   Lord Chi K'ang asked Confucius about governing, and Confucius said: "Utter rectitude is utter government. If you let rectitude lead the people, how could anyone fail to be rectified?"

18   Lord Chi K'ang was having trouble with bandits. When he asked Confucius for advice, Confucius said: "If you weren't so full of desire yourself, you couldn't pay people to steal from you."

19   Asking Confucius about governing, Lord Chi K'ang said: "What if I secure those who abide in the Way by killing those who ignore the Way – will that work?"

"How can you govern by killing?" replied Confucius. "Just set your heart on what is virtuous and benevolent, and the people will be virtuous and benevolent. The noble-minded have the Integrity of wind, and little people the Integrity of grass. When the wind sweeps over grass, it bends."

20   Adept Chang asked: "What must a man be like before he is pronounced influential?"

"What on earth do you mean by *influential?*" countered the Master.

"*Influential* means a person who gains renown among the people and the great families," replied Chang.

"But that's only renown," said the Master, "not influence. A person of influence is, by nature, forthright and a lover of Duty. He weighs people's words carefully and studies their faces. He cultivates humility before others. Such a person infuses the people and great families with his influence.

"A person of renown makes a show of Humanity, but acts quite differently. And he never doubts himself. That is the kind of person who gains renown among the people and the great families."

21   Out wandering with the Master near Rain-Dance Altar, Fan Ch'ih said: "May I ask about *exalting Integrity, reforming depravity,* and *unraveling delusion?*"

"A splendid question!" replied the Master. "To serve first, and let the rewards follow as they will – is that not exalting Integrity? To attack evil itself, not the evil person – is that not reforming depravity? To endanger yourself and your family, all in a morning's blind rage – is that not delusion?"

22   Fan Ch'ih asked about Humanity, and the Master said: "Love people."

Then he asked about understanding, and the Master said: "Understand people."

Fan Ch'ih couldn't fathom what he meant, so the Master said: "If you raise up the straight and cast out the crooked, the crooked will be made straight."

After leaving, Fan Ch'ih went to visit Adept Hsia, and said: "I was just visiting the Master. I asked him about understanding, and he said: *If you raise up the straight and cast out the crooked, the crooked will be made straight.* What does he mean by that?"

"O, there's such bounty in those words," replied Hsia. "When Shun possessed all beneath Heaven, he recognized Kao Yao and raised him up, thus leaving those without Humanity far away. And when T'ang[5] possessed all beneath Heaven, he recognized Yi Yin and raised him up, thus leaving those without Humanity far away."

23   Adept Hsia asked about friends, and the Master said: "Advise them faithfully in perfecting the Way. If that fails, then stop. Don't humiliate yourself."

24   Master Tseng said: "The noble-minded use cultivation to assemble their friends, and friends to sustain their Humanity."

月想果一士　　　　　
氏陵立延是　　　　　
聖心於扵仁　　　　　
嬰念禮玄間　　　　　
真器器君　　　　　
希家樂以同　　　　　
元宮之注權　　　　　
魯昔世昔敬　　　　　
百親禮荷　　　　　
王里樂鐘　　　　　
并官陵陵　　　　　
官改遲

XIII   Adept Lu

1 Adept Lu asked about governing, and the Master said: "Put the people first, and reward their efforts well."

When Lu asked further, he said: "Never tire."

2 When he was a regent for the House of Chi, Jan Yung asked about governing, and the Master said: "Depend on the lesser officials. Forgive their minor offenses and raise up worthy talents."

"How will I recognize worthy talents and raise them up?"

"If you raise up those you recognize," replied the Master, "do you think people will let you ignore those you don't recognize?"

3 Adept Lu said: "If the Lord of Wei wanted you to govern his country, what would you put first in importance?"

"The rectification of names," replied the Master. "Without a doubt."

"That's crazy!" countered Lu. ""What does rectification have to do with anything?"

"You're such an uncivil slob," said the Master. "When the noble-minded can't understand something, they remain silent.

"Listen. If names aren't rectified, speech doesn't follow from reality. If speech doesn't follow from reality, endeavors never come to fruition. If endeavors never come to fruition, then Ritual and music cannot flourish. If Ritual and music cannot flourish, punishments don't fit the crime. If punishments don't fit the crime, people can't put their hands and feet anywhere without fear of losing them.[1]

"Naming enables the noble-minded to speak, and speech enables the noble-minded to act. Therefore, the noble-minded are anything but careless in speech."

4   Fan Ch'ih asked to learn about farming, and the Master said: "Any old farmer could teach you that better than me."

Then Fan Ch'ih asked to learn about growing vegetables, and the Master said: "And any old gardener could teach you that better than me."

After Fan Ch'ih left, the Master said: "Fan Ch'ih's such a small-minded person! If leaders love Ritual, the people cannot be anything but reverent. If leaders love Duty, the people cannot be anything but humble. If leaders love standing by their words, the people cannot be anything but sincere. Once this is done, people from all four corners of the earth will come carrying babies wrapped on their backs. So why is he worried about farming?"

5   The Master said: "A man may be able to chant all three hundred *Songs* from memory, and still falter when appointed to office or waver when sent on embassies to the four corners of the earth. What good are all those *Songs* if he can't put them to use?"

6   The Master said: "A ruler who has rectified himself never gives orders, and all goes well. A ruler who has not rectified himself gives orders, and the people never follow them."

7   The Master said: "These two states, Lu and Wei: in politics, they're like brothers."

8   Of Ching, son to the Duke of Wei, the Master said: "He lived in his house nobly. When he moved in, he said: *Quite nice.* When he made it comfortable, he said: *Quite adequate.* And when it was lavishly appointed, he said: *Quite beautiful.*"

9   The Master journeyed to Wei with Jan Ch'iu driving for him. When they arrived, the Master said: "So many people!"

"Once a people has flourished like this," said Jan Ch'iu, "what more could be done for them?"

"Give them prosperity."

"And once they grow prosperous, what then?"

"Educate them."

10   The Master said: "If someone employed me for even a single year, a great deal could be done. And in three years, the work could be complete."

11   The Master said: "They say: *If a country had wise rulers for a hundred years, violence would be conquered and killing vanquished.* And it's so true."

12   The Master said: "Even if a true Emperor arose, it would still take a generation – but then Humanity would rule."

13   The Master said: "Once you've rectified yourself, you can serve in government without difficulty. But if you haven't rectified yourself, how can you rectify the people?"

14   Jan Ch'iu returned from the Chi family's royal court, and the Master said: "Why so late?"

"Urgent government business."

"It must have been family business," replied the Master. "I may not hold any office, but I would have been consulted if it were really government business."

15   Duke Ting asked if there is a precept that could lead a country to prosperity, and the Master said: "Precepts cannot do such things. But they say: *To be a ruler is difficult indeed, and to be a subject is hardly easy.* If a man understands how difficult it is to rule, isn't that close to a single precept leading a country to prosperity?"

"Is there a precept that could destroy a country?" asked the Duke.

"Precepts cannot do such things. But they say: *In ruling, there is but one joy: no one dares defy you*. If a ruler is good and no one dares defy him, isn't that good? But if a ruler is evil and no one dares defy him, isn't that close to a single precept destroying an entire country?"

16   Duke She asked about governing, and the Master said: "When those nearby are pleased, those far away come and gather round."

17   When he was regent in Chü Fu, Adept Hsia asked about governing, and the Master said: "Don't rush things, and don't think about small gains. If you rush around, your efforts will lead nowhere. If you worry about small gains, your great endeavors will go unrealized."

18   Speaking to Confucius, the Duke She said: "In my village there was a man called BodyUpright. When his father stole a sheep, he testified against him."

"In my village," said Confucius, "to be upright was something else altogether. Fathers harbored sons, and sons harbored fathers – and between them, they were upright."

19   Fan Ch'ih asked about Humanity, and the Master said: "Dwell at home in humility. Conduct your business in reverence. And in your dealings with others, be faithful.

"Even if you go east or north to live among wild tribes, these are things you must never disregard."

20   Adept Kung asked: "To be called a noble official, what must a person be like?"

"Always conducting himself with a sense of shame," replied the Master, "and when sent on embassies to the four corners of the earth, never disgracing his sovereign's commission – such a person can be called a noble official."

"May I ask about those in the next lower rank?"

"Their family elders praise them as filial children," replied the Master, "and their fellow villagers praise them as brothers."

"May I ask about those in the next rank?"

"They always stand by their words and bring their undertakings to completion. They may be stubborn, small-minded people, but still they can be accorded the next rank."

"And those who are running the government now – what do you think of them?" asked Kung.

"Nothing but utensils!" sighed the Master. "Peck-and-hamper people too small even to measure."

21　The Master said: "I can't find students who steer the middle course, so I turn to the impetuous and the timid. The impetuous forge ahead, and the timid know what to avoid."

22　The Master said: "In the south it is said: *Without constancy, people cannot be shamans or doctors.* That says it well."

Integrity without constancy brings disgrace.[2] "Yes, yes," commented the Master, "you don't need a fortune-teller to see that!"

23　The Master said: "A noble-minded person is different from others, but at peace with them. A small-minded person is the same as others, but never at peace with them."

24 Adept Kung asked: "What do you think of *All the villagers love him?*"

"That is not enough," replied the Master.

"What do you think of *All the villagers hate him?*"

"That isn't enough either. It should be: *All the good villagers love him, and all the evil villagers hate him.*"

25 The Master said: "The noble-minded are easy to serve, but difficult to please. If you ignore the Way in trying to please them, they won't be pleased. But they recognize the limits of those who serve them.

"Little people are difficult to serve, but easy to please. If you ignore the Way in trying to please them, they'll be pleased nonetheless. And they demand perfection from those who serve them."

26 The Master said: "The noble-minded are·stately, but never arrogant. Little people are arrogant, but never stately."

27 The Master said: "Enduring, resolute, simple, slow to speak – that's nearly Humanity."

28   Adept Lu asked: "To be called a noble official, what must a person be like?"

"Earnest and exacting, but also genial," replied the Master. "Such a person can be called a noble official. Earnest and exacting with friends, genial with brothers."

29   The Master said: "The people should be broadly educated by a wise teacher for seven years – then they can take up the weapons of war."

30   The Master said: "Sending people to war without educating them first: that is called *throwing the people away*."

月□寶俱製元道百王不改
顏氏聖舅家居魯親里并官
尊孔心念聖歷世禮樂陵遲
造立禮器樂之音符鍾磬瑟
宣抒玄汙以注水流法舊不
士仁聞君風耀敬咏其德尊

XIV   Yüan Szu Asked About

1   Yüan Szu asked about disgrace, and the Master said: "To enjoy a salary when your country abides in the Way – that is fine. But to enjoy a salary when your country ignores the Way – that is a disgrace."

"Never domineering or arrogant, free of resentment and desire – is that Humanity?" asked Yüan.

"It's certainly difficult," replied the Master. "But I don't know if it's Humanity."

2   The Master said: "A thinker who cherishes the comforts of home isn't much of a thinker."

3   The Master said: "When your country abides in the Way, let your words and actions be daring. When your country ignores the Way, let your actions be daring and your words cautious."

4   The Master said: "Masters of Integrity are sure to be well-spoken, but the well-spoken aren't necessarily masters of Integrity. The Humane are sure to be courageous, but the courageous aren't necessarily Humane."

5   Speaking to Confucius, Nan-kung Kuo asked: "Yi was a mighty archer and Ao could push a boat over dry land, but neither of these legendary warriors lived out their full years. Yü and Chi, on the other hand, devoted themselves to farming and inherited all beneath Heaven in the end."[1]

The Master said nothing.

After Nan-kung Kuo had left, the Master said: "How truly noble-minded he is! And O, how deeply he reveres Integrity!"

6   The Master said: "The noble-minded may not always be Humane. But the small-minded – they never are."

7   The Master said: "How can you love people without encouraging them? And how can you be loyal to people without educating them?"

8   The Master said: "To compose a royal communiqué – P'i Ch'en first drafted the text; Shih Shu reviewed and discussed it; Lord Yü, the minister of foreign embassies, revised and polished it; and finally, Prime Minister Ch'an filled it with beauty."

9   Someone asked about Prime Minister Ch'an, and the Master said: "He was generous."

Asked about Prime Minister Hsi, the Master said: "O, that one! That one!"

Asked about Kuan Chung, the Master said: "In Pien, he seized the Po family's three hundred villages, but even though the family was reduced to eating meager fare, they never uttered a word of resentment. That's what kind of person he was."

10   The Master said: "To be poor and free of resentment is difficult. To be rich and free of arrogance is easy."

11   The Master said: "Meng Kung-ch'uo[2] would have been fine as senior advisor for some family like Chao or Wei,[3] but not as high minister for an actual country, even a tiny one like T'eng or Hsüeh."

12   Adept Lu asked about the realized person, and the Master said: "One who possesses Tsang Wu-chung's wisdom, Meng Kung-ch'uo's desirelessness, Master Chuang of Pien's courage, and Jan Ch'iu's accomplishments, and who refines these virtues with Ritual and music – that is a realized person.

"But," he added, "perhaps it isn't necessary to ask so much of a realized person these days. If you think of Duty upon seeing profit, risk your life upon seeing danger, and maintain your principles through long hardship – then you, too, are a realized person."

13 Asking Kung-ming Chia about Kung-shu Wen-tzu,[4] the Master said: "Is it really true that your master never spoke, never laughed, and never chose?"

"Whoever told you that was wrong," replied Kung-ming. "The Master spoke only at the proper time, so people never tired of his words. He laughed only when he was happy, so people never tired of his laugh. And he chose only what was right, so people never tired of his choices."

"If that's who he was," responded the Master, "then who was he?"

14 The Master said: "On his way into exile, Tsang Wu-chung[5] occupied his ancestral lands, insisting that the Lu duke leave it in the hands of his family. People may say this wasn't coercion, but I don't believe it."

15 The Master said: "Duke Wen of Chin was scheming and not at all upright. Duke Huan of Ch'i, on the other hand, was upright and not at all scheming."

16 Adept Lu said: "When Duke Huan[6] had his brother, Chiu, put to death, Shao Hu died trying to save Chiu, but Kuan Chung did not."

"In this," he added, "Kuan Chung fell short of Humanity, did he not?"

"It was Kuan Chung's strength that allowed Duke Huan to unite the nine lords without force, and so save the empire," replied the Master. "What Humanity! What amazing Humanity!"

17 Adept Kung said: "Kuan Chung was hardly Humane, was he? He didn't die trying to save Chiu when Duke Huan had him put to death – in fact, he became Huan's Prime Minister!"

"As Prime Minister, Kuan Chung enabled Huan to lead the nine lords and unite all beneath Heaven," replied the Master. "Even today, our people still enjoy the blessings he bestowed. If it weren't for him, we'd still let our hair hang loose and button our robes to the left like barbarians.

"Why should such a man commit suicide out in some ditch, with no one the wiser, all in blind obedience to the small fidelities of commoners?"

18 Chuan was a retainer in Kung-shu Wen-tzu's household. Later, he was promoted to a high state office, becoming Kung-shu Wen-tzu's colleague. Hearing of this, the Master said: "Wen:[7] a name well-chosen indeed."

19 The Master was talking about how Duke Ling of Wei had so completely ignored the Way, when Lord Chi K'ang asked: "If that's true, how is it he never came to grief?"

"He trusted foreign affairs to Lord K'ung Wen," replied Confucius, "his ancestral temple to Priest T'o, and his military to Wang-sun Chia. So how could he come to grief?"[8]

20 The Master said: "Immodest words are not easily put into action."

21 When Ch'en Heng[9] assassinated Duke Chien, Confucius bathed according to Ritual and went to court. There, informing Duke Ai, he said: "Ch'en Heng has assassinated his sovereign. I would encourage you to punish him."

"Inform the three family leaders," said the duke.

"I only inform you of such things," replied Confucius,

"because I serve under the high ministers, and it is therefore my duty. Now you say *Inform the three family leaders*?"

He thereupon went to inform the three family leaders. When they refused to take action against Ch'en Heng, he said: "I only inform you of such things because I serve under the high ministers, and it is therefore my duty."

22 Adept Lu asked about serving a sovereign, and the Master said: "If you challenge his decisions, do it with honest loyalty."

23 The Master said: "The noble-minded influence those above them. Little people influence those below them."

24 The Master said: "The ancients studied in order to rule themselves. These days, people study in order to rule others."

25 C‍h'ü Po-yü[10] sent an emissary to see Confucius. Once they were seated, Confucius asked: "What is your master working on?"

"He's trying to reduce his faults," replied the man, "but he isn't having much luck."

After the emissary left, the Master said: "What an emissary! What an amazing emissary!"

26 The Master said: "Unless you've been appointed to office, don't fuss and fret over the business of government."

And Master Tseng added: "The noble-minded always keep to their place, even in their thoughts."

27 The Master said: "The noble-minded say little and achieve much."

28 The Master said: "The Way of a noble-minded person has three facets, all of which are beyond me: the

Humane have no worries; the wise have no doubts; and the courageous have no fear."

"But that," protested Adept Kung, "is precisely the Way you've mastered."

29   Adept Kung was forever comparing and criticizing people. The Master said: "To have time for such things, Kung must have already perfected himself completely! As for me, I am not so lucky."

30   The Master said: "Don't grieve when people fail to recognize your ability. Grieve for your lack of ability instead."

31   The Master said: "One who never anticipates deceit or expects duplicity, and yet is the first to recognize such things – is that not a sage indeed?"

32   Wang-sheng Mu said to Confucius: "Why all this anxious equivocation? It isn't that you're only trying to please people, is it?"

"No, it isn't that," replied Confucius. "It's just that I can't bear stubborn self-righteousness."

33   The Master said: "A legendary horse is praised not for its strength, but for its Integrity."

34   Someone asked: "What do you think of *Answer resentment with Integrity?*"

"Then how do you answer *Integrity?*" responded the Master. "Answer resentment with justice, and use Integrity to answer Integrity."

35   The Master said: "No one's ever understood me."

"Why not?" asked Adept Kung.

"I never resent Heaven or blame people," replied the Master. "In learning the ways of this world, I've fathomed Heaven. So perhaps Heaven, at least, understands me."

36   Speaking to Chi Sun,[11] Kung-po Liao[12] slandered Adept Lu. Telling the Master of this, Tzu-fu Ching-po[13] said: "My master's been taken in by these deceits. But I still have the power to add Kung-po's corpse to the market's display of criminals."

"When the Way abides, it's destiny," said the Master. "And when the Way's cast aside, it's destiny. How could Kung-po Liao alter destiny?"

37   The Master said: "A sage is one who lives beyond his day and age. Next come those who live beyond the place they inhabit. After that, those who live beyond beauty. And after that, those who live beyond words."

The Master said: "There have been only seven."

38   Adept Lu spent a night at Stone Gate, and the gatekeeper asked: "Where are you from?"

"From the House of Confucius," replied Lu.

"Isn't he the one who knows it's hopeless, but keeps trying anyway?"

39   The Master was playing stone chimes at the house where he was staying in Wei. Just then, a passerby carrying a basket stopped at the gate and said: "There's so much passion in that music!"

Then he quickly added: "So much petty urgency in all that stubborn clacking! If no one understands you, then that's that.

> When it's deep – you wade through, clothes and all.
> When it's shallow – you lift your robes and step
>   across."[14]

"Of course!" said the Master. "Anything else would be difficult indeed!"

40   Adept Chang said: *"The Book of History says Kao Tsung[15] kept to his mourning hut for three years and never spoke. What does this mean?"*

"Why single out Kao Tsung?" replied the Master. "The ancients were all like that. When a sovereign died, the hundred officers all joined together and for three years trusted government to the Prime Minister."

41   The Master said: "If leaders love Ritual, the people will be easy to rule."

42   Adept Lu asked about the noble-minded, and the Master said: "They cultivate themselves, and so master reverence."

"Is that all it takes?" asked Lu.

"They cultivate themselves, and so bring peace to others."

"Is that all it takes?"

"They cultivate themselves, and so bring peace to the people. If you cultivate yourself, and so bring peace to the people, how could even Yao or Shun criticize you?"

43   Yüan Jang sat waiting on his haunches.

When he arrived, the Master said: "Showing no deference or respect when young, accomplishing nothing worth handing down when grown, and refusing to die when old – such people are nothing but pests."

At that, flicking his walking-stick, the Master cracked Yüan on the shin.

44 A boy from Ch'üeh Village had been hired as the Master's messenger. Asking about him, someone said: "Is he making progress?"

"I've seen him sit and walk among his elders," replied the Master, "as if he were already their equal. He has no interest in making progress. He wants it all right now."

顒月氏聖婆家帝元魯親里百王不改官

仁挧立阮心念其唇世禮樂弄宮

聞玄禮聖念家韋元魯親里王不

君汙器念真家唇魯世禮樂弄陵

局以弟遷盧曾世禮陵遲

權注之譽普世待禮鐘磬陵遲

敬水普世待豐樂陵

卜沈深待鐘磬

具海鐘磬樂陵

xv Duke Ling of Wei

1   Duke Ling of Wei asked Confucius about tactics, and Confucius said: "I've learned something about the conduct of worship and sacrifice. But as for the conduct of war – that is something I've never studied."

2   Confucius left the next day.

In Ch'en, when supplies ran out, the disciples grew so weak they couldn't get to their feet. Adept Lu, his anger flaring, asked: "How is it the noble-minded must endure such privation?"

"If you're noble-minded, you're resolute in privation," the Master replied. "Little people get swept away."

3   The Master said: "Kung, do you think of me as someone who studies widely and remembers what he learns?"

"Yes," replied Adept Kung. "Aren't you?"

"No. I've just found a single thread stringing it all together."[1]

4   The Master said: "Those who understand Integrity are rare indeed, Lu."

5   The Master said: "If anyone has managed to rule by doing nothing,[2] surely it was Shun. And how did he do so much by doing nothing? He just sat reverently facing south,[3] that's all!"

6   Adept Chang asked about action, and the Master said: "If you stand by your words, and they're loyal, your actions will be reverent and true. Then you can put your words into action, even in a barbarian country. But if you don't stand by your words, and they aren't loyal, your actions won't be reverent and true. Then how could you ever put your words into action, even in your own neighborhood?

"Keep this precept before you, even when standing or riding, and you'll make your words into actions."

Thereupon Adept Chang wrote it on his sash.

7   The Master said: "How straight and true Shih Yü[4] is! When the country abides in the Way, he's true as an arrow.

And when the country ignores the Way, he's still true as an arrow.

"How noble-minded Ch'ü Po-yü is! When the country abides in the Way, he takes office. And when the country ignores the Way, he hides himself away and embraces it alone."

8   The Master said: "When a person is capable of understanding your words, and you refuse to speak, you're wasting a person. When a person isn't capable of understanding your words, and you speak anyway, you're wasting words. The wise waste neither words nor people."

9   The Master said: "As for noble officers of purpose and Humanity – they never wound Humanity to secure life. Indeed, to perfect Humanity, they often endure death."

10   Adept Kung asked about the practice of Humanity, and the Master said: "If a craftsman wants to do good work, he must first sharpen his tools. If you want to settle in a country, you must cultivate its wise ministers and befriend its Humane officials."

11   Yen Hui asked about governing a country, and the Master said: "Follow the Hsia's dynastic calendar, ride the Shang's dynastic carriage, wear the Chou's dynastic cap, and for music, choose the music of Emperors Shun and Wu. Banish the songs of Cheng, and send clever tongues far away. The songs of Cheng are dissolute and clever tongues a peril."

12   The Master said: "If things far away don't concern you, you'll soon mourn things close at hand."

13   The Master said: "It's all over. I've never seen anyone for whom loving Integrity is like loving a beautiful woman."

14   The Master said: "Tsang Wen-chung stole his high position, didn't he? He knew how wise and worthy Liu-hsia Hui[5] was, and yet didn't offer the position to him."

15   The Master said: "If you expect great things of yourself and demand little of others, you'll keep resentment far away."

16   The Master said: "There's nothing to be done for a person who isn't constantly asking *What should be done? What should be done?*"

17   The Master said: "For people to talk all day, enthralled with their clever chitchat, and never once mention right or wrong – that must be difficult indeed!"

18   The Master said: "The noble-minded make Duty their very nature. They put it into practice through Ritual; they make it shine through humility; and standing by their words, they perfect it. Then they are noble-minded indeed!"

19   The Master said: "The noble-minded worry about their lack of ability, not about people's failure to recognize their ability."

20   The Master said: "Leaving a name that carries no honor through the ages following their death – that is what the noble-minded dread."

21   The Master said: "The noble-minded seek within themselves. Little people seek elsewhere."

22   The Master said: "The noble-minded stand above the fray with dignity. And when they band together with others, they never lose track of themselves."

23   The Master said: "The noble-minded don't honor a person because of something he's said, nor do they dismiss something said because of the person who said it."

24   Adept Kung asked: "Is there any one word that could guide a person throughout life?"

The Master replied: "How about *'shu': never impose on others what you would not choose for yourself*?"

25 The Master said: "Who have I condemned, and who praised? If there are those I have praised, it's easy enough to test them: for it was through the people that the Three Dynasties[6] put this straight Way into practice, and the people are no different today."

26 The Master said: "I can remember when scribes would leave a blank space if they weren't sure of a character, and people would loan their horses to friends. But that's all over now."

27 The Master said: "Clever talk ruins Integrity, and even a little impatience can ruin great plans."

28 The Master said: "When everyone hates a person, you should investigate thoroughly. And when everyone loves a person, you should also investigate thoroughly."

29 The Master said: "People can make the Way great and vast. But the Way isn't what makes people great and vast."

30   The Master said: "To be wrong without trying to change, that is called *wrong* indeed."

31   The Master said: "I've spent days without food and nights without sleep, hoping to purify thought and clarify mind. But it's never done much good. Such practices – they're nothing like devoted study."

32   The Master said: "The noble-minded devote themselves to the Way, not to earning a living. A farmer may go hungry, and a scholar may stumble into a good salary. So it is that the noble-minded worry about the Way, not poverty and hunger."

33   The Master said: "You may understand it, but if you can't sustain it with Humanity, it will slip from your grasp.

"You may understand it and sustain it with Humanity, but if you don't govern with solemn dignity, there'll be no reverence among the people.

"You may understand it, sustain it with Humanity, and govern with solemn dignity, but if you don't put it into practice according to Ritual, no good will come of it."

34   The Master said: "The noble-minded aren't easily known, but they're worthy of great responsibilities. The small-minded aren't worthy of great responsibilities, but they're easily known."

35   The Master said: "Humanity is more essential to the people than fire and water. I've seen people die trying to purify themselves by walking through fire or over water. But I've never seen anyone die because they've walked in Humanity."

36   The Master said: "Abide in Humanity, and you need not defer to any teacher."

37   The Master said: "The noble-minded are principled, but never dogmatic."

38   The Master said: "In serving your sovereign, be reverent about your duties and casual about your salary."

39   The Master said: "In worthy teaching, all things are related."[7]

40   The Master said: "If you don't follow the same Way, don't make plans together."

41   The Master said: "Language is insight itself."

42   Music-master Mien[8] arrived for a visit. When he reached the steps, the Master said: "Here are the steps."

Leading him to the mat, the Master said: "Here's the mat."

Once they were seated, the Master told him: "So-and-so is here. So-and-so is there. . . ."

After Music-master Mien left, Adept Chang asked: "Talking like this to a master musician – is that the Way?"

"Yes," replied the Master. "With a master musician, that is indeed the Way."

顧氏聖心，念真之世，禮樂鍾陵遲

昊立心念真之世禮樂鍾陵

足禮器樂之普世待建馨陵

是仁玄汙水注水深港

十仁聞君同種教

月幸元百主不改

家石魯親里弃官

XVI   The House of Chi

I   The House of Chi was about to attack Chuan-yü.[1] Jan Ch'iu and Adept Lu went to see Confucius and said: "Our Lord Chi is about to settle things with Chuan-yü."

"Aren't you to blame for this?" responded Confucius. "Long ago, the early Emperors put Chuan-yü in charge of worship and sacrifice at Tung-meng Mountain. And besides, it's part of our own territory: its rulers serve these same gods of earth and grain. How can Chi think of attacking them?"

"It's our master's wish," replied Jan Ch'iu, "not ours."

"Chou Jen had a saying: *The capable join forces; the incapable step aside.* What good are counselors who don't steady him when he's stumbling and support him when he's falling? And besides, what you say is wrong. Isn't someone to blame if tigers and wild bulls escape from their cages, or jewelry of tortoiseshell and jade is crushed in its box?"

"But Chuan-yü has grown very strong," said Jan Ch'iu, "and it's so near the Chi capital. If it isn't dealt with now, it will terrorize the Chi descendants for ages to come."

"The noble-minded can't bear people who hedge around instead of saying what they want," countered Confucius.

"This is what I've learned: leaders of countries and noble houses don't worry about having too few people, they worry about equitable rule; and they don't worry about the people living in poverty, they worry about the people living in peace. If rule is equitable, there's no poverty. If there's harmony, there's no lack of people. And if there's peace, there's no rebellion.

"If a ruler's like this, and people in far-off lands still don't turn to him, he cultivates his Integrity to attract them. And after they're attracted, he brings them peace.

"Now you two are this man's high counselors. People in far-off lands haven't turned to him, but you haven't shown him how to attract them. And the country's falling into utter ruins, but you haven't shown him how to preserve it. Instead, you're busy plotting war against your own country! If you want to know what will terrorize the descendants of Chi, don't go looking for it in Chuan-yü: look for it in the palace of Lord Chi himself."

2   Confucius said: "When all beneath Heaven abides in the Way – Ritual, music, and war all emanate from the Son of Heaven.

"When all beneath Heaven ignores the Way – Ritual, music, and war emanate from lords and princes. It's rare for such a nation to outlast ten generations. If they emanate from state ministers, it's rare for a nation to outlast five generations. And once officials start issuing imperial commands, it's rare for a nation to outlast three generations.

"When all beneath Heaven abides in the Way, governing is not left to ministers. And when all beneath Heaven abides in the Way, common people need not discuss politics."

3   Confucius said: "It's been five generations since the Lu rulers lost control of the treasury, and four generations since state ministers took control of the government. No wonder these descendants of the Three Families are in such decline!"

4   Confucius said: "There are three kinds of friends that bring profit, and three kinds that bring ruin. Forthright friends, trustworthy friends, well-informed friends: these bring profit. Obsequious friends, compliant friends, clever-tongued friends: these bring ruin."

5   Confucius said: "There are three kinds of joy that bring profit, and three kinds that bring ruin. The joy of

following Ritual and music, the joy of praising people's virtue and benevolence, the joy of having many wise friends: these bring profit. The joy of extravagant pleasures, the joy of dissolute living, the joy of convivial pleasures: these bring ruin."

6   Confucius said: "In serving a noble-minded leader, there are three common mistakes: speaking without being asked, which is called impetuous; refusing to speak after being asked, which is called aloof; speaking without considering his demeanor, which is called blindness."

7   Confucius said: "The noble-minded guard against three things: in youth, when *ch'i* and blood are unsettled, they guard against beautiful women; in their prime, when *ch'i* and blood are unbending, they guard against belligerence; and in old age, when *ch'i* and blood are withering, they guard against avarice."

8   Confucius said: "The noble-minded stand in awe of three things: the Mandate of Heaven, great men, and the words of a sage. Little people don't understand the Mandate

of Heaven, so they aren't awed by it. They scorn great men, and they ridicule the words of a sage."

9   Confucius said: "To be born enlightened: that is highest. To study and so become enlightened: that is next. To feel trapped and so study: that is third. To feel trapped and never study: that is the level of the common people, the lowest level."

10   Confucius said: "The noble-minded have nine states of mind: for eyes, bright; for ears, penetrating; for countenance, cordial; for demeanor, humble; for words, trustworthy; for service, reverent; for doubt, questioning; for anger, circumspect; and for facing a chance to profit, moral."

11   Confucius said: "*I clutch good as if it were eluding me, and touch evil as if testing hot water:* I have seen such people and heard such claims.

"*I live as a recluse to realize my aspirations, and put Duty into practice to extend the Way's influence:* I have heard such claims, but never seen such people."

₁₂ Duke Ching of Ch'i had a thousand teams of horses, but when he died the people couldn't find a single excuse to praise him. But Po Yi and Shu Ch'i starved below Shou-yang Mountain, and the people praise them to this day.

Isn't that what this means?[2]

₁₃ Asking of Po-yü, the son of Confucius, Adept Ch'in said: "You must have learned things we've never been taught."

"No," replied Po-yü. "Once, when my father was standing alone, I was crossing the courtyard. I was hurrying, out of reverence, but he stopped me and asked: *Have you studied the* Songs? When I told him that I hadn't, he said: *Unless you study the* Songs, *you'll have nothing to say.* I withdrew and began studying the *Songs.*

"Another day, he was standing alone again. And again I was hurrying reverently across the courtyard, when he asked: *Have you studied Ritual?* When I told him that I hadn't, he said: *Unless you study Ritual, you'll have nowhere to stand.* I withdrew and began studying Ritual.

"These are the two things I have learned."

Adept Ch'in withdrew in delight, and said: "One question,

three answers! I've learned about the *Songs*. I've learned about Ritual. And I've learned that a noble-minded man keeps his son at a distance."

14 The true sovereign calls his wife *lady*. The lady calls herself *little girl*. The people call her *our lord's lady*. But when visiting other countries, they call her *our little lord*. And people in other countries also call her *our lord's lady*.

月氏聖聰家希元　　百主不改官
顏氏　心念　魯親里并
興立於　世禮樂陵
迁禮器　晉待鍾
旦將互浮以　水濟
一仁聞君同　　敬　思
歷　仁

XVII Yang Huo

$_1$ Yang Huo[1] wanted to visit Confucius, but Confucius refused to see him. So he sent a piglet to Confucius as a gift. Choosing a time Yang would be out, Confucius went to offer the obligatory thanks at Yang's house. But on his way there he met Yang on the street.

"Come," Yang said, "I must speak with you.

"If a man keeps his treasure hidden away while chaos engulfs his country, can he be called Humane? Of course not. And if a man longs for public life but lets the opportunity slip away again and again, can he be called wise? Of course not.

"Days and months are slipping away. The years are not on our side."

"Alright," replied Confucius reluctantly, "I'm ready to take office."

$_2$ The Master said: "We're all the same by nature. It's living that makes us so different."

3 The Master said: "Those of the loftiest wisdom and those of the basest ignorance: they alone never change."

4 The Master went to Wu-ch'eng,[2] and there heard the music of voices and strings. Well-pleased, the Master smiled and said: "What good is a big ox-cleaver when killing chickens?"

"Long ago," replied Adept Yu, "I heard you say: *When the noble-minded study the Way, they love people. When little people study the Way, they're easy to employ.*"

"My disciples," said the Master, "what Yu says is right. What I said before – that was only a joke."

5 When Kung-shan Fu-jao[3] rebelled against the House of Chi and took its capital, he summoned the Master. The Master was ready to go, but Adept Lu was very unhappy and said: "You, who never answer such calls – why go to this Kung-shan?"

"He couldn't have summoned me for nothing," replied the Master. "And if he really employs me, I can re-create our glorious Chou in the east."

6   Adept Chang asked about Humanity, and Confucius said: "There are five essentials. If you can put them into practice throughout all beneath Heaven, then you've mastered Humanity."

"What are they?"

"Reverence, broad-mindedness, sincerity, diligence, and generosity. Reverent, and so never scorned; broad-minded, and so winning over the people; sincere, and so trusted; diligent, and so accomplishing much; generous, and so served willingly."

7   Pi Hsi[4] summoned the Master, and the Master was ready to go. Adept Lu said: "I once heard you say: *The noble-minded never enter the country of a man who chooses evil of his own accord.* This Pi Hsi has rebelled against the House of Chao and taken the city of Chung-mou. How can you think of going to him?"

"Yes, I did say that," replied the Master. "But is it not said: *Hard indeed: a grindstone cannot wear it away*? And is it not said: *White indeed: black mud cannot darken it*?

"Am I to be a bitter gourd, left dangling on a string and never eaten?"

8   The Master asked: "Have you heard the six precepts and their six deceptions?"

"No," replied Adept Lu.

"Then sit, and I'll tell you," said the Master. "To love Humanity without loving learning: that's the deception of foolishness. To love wisdom without loving learning: that's the deception of dissipation. To love sincerity without loving learning: that's the deception of subterfuge. To love veracity without loving learning: that's the deception of intolerance. To love courage without loving learning: that's the deception of confusion. And to love determination without loving learning: that's the deception of recklessness."

9   The Master said: "How is it, my little ones, that none of you study the *Songs*? Through the *Songs*, you can inspire people and turn their gaze inward, bring people together and give voice to their grievances. Through them you serve your father when home and your sovereign when away, and you learn the names of countless birds and animals and plants."

Then the Master said to his son, Po-yü: "Have you worked through the *Chou Nan* and the *Shao Nan*?[5] Until you've worked through at least them, you'll live as if you stood facing a wall."

10   The Master said: "When I keep saying *Ritual! Ritual!,* do you think I'm just ranting about jade and silk? And when I keep saying *Music! Music!,* do you think I'm just ranting about bells and drums?"

11   The Master said: "Some act fierce and determined, but inside they're cowards. What little people – like petty thieves stealing into courtyards!"

12   The Master said: "A righteous villager is the thief of Integrity."

13   The Master said: "To hear the Way[6] and speak in muddy alleys – that is to cast away Integrity."

14   The Master said: "How can you take such squalid little people for colleagues and still serve your sovereign? They worry constantly about getting what they want. Once they get it, they worry about losing it. And once they start that, there's nothing they won't do."

15   The Master said: "In ancient times, the people had three weaknesses. Now they rarely even have those. The impetuous were once unrestrained – now they're full of reckless abandon. The proud were once dignified – now they're full of angry indignation. The foolish were once true – now they're full of cunning guile."

16   The Master said: "Clever tongues and fawning looks: such people are rarely Humane."

17   The Master said: "I hate to see purple replacing the purity of vermilion. I hate to see those dissolute songs of Cheng confused with the stately music of Ya.[7] And I hate to see calculating tongues pitching countries and noble houses into ruin."

18   The Master said: "I'd love to just say nothing."

    "But if you say nothing," said Adept Kung, "how would we disciples hand down your teachings?"

    "What has Heaven ever said?" replied the Master. "The four seasons keep turning and the hundred things keep emerging – but what has Heaven ever said?"

19   Ju Pei wanted to visit Confucius. Confucius declined, using illness as an excuse. But he picked up his *se* as the messenger was leaving and sang – loud enough that the messenger was sure to hear.

20   Tsai Yü asked about the three-year mourning period: "Surely one year is long enough. If the noble-minded ignore Ritual for three years, Ritual will be in ruins. And if they ignore music for three years, music will be a shambles. Old grain used up, new grain sprouting, and spring's Ritual fires replacing winter's: surely a year is enough."

"So," replied the Master, "by now you're content eating fancy rice and wearing fine brocade?"

"Yes."

"Well, if you're content, then go ahead. For the noble-minded in mourning, there's no savor in food and no joy in music. There's no contentment in their homes, so they don't eat fancy rice or wear fine brocade. But if you're content, you should go ahead and enjoy yourself."

After Tsai Yü left, the Master said: "How Inhumane Yü is! A child spends its first three years in the nurturing arms of its parents. That's why the mourning period lasts three years throughout all beneath Heaven. Didn't Yü also enjoy his parents' loving arms for three years?"

21   The Master said: "All day eating and never thinking: such people are serious trouble. Aren't there games to play, like *go* and chess? Even that is better than nothing."

22   Adept Kung asked: "The noble-minded revere courage, don't they?"

"The noble-minded honor Duty above all," replied the Master. "In the noble-minded, courage without Duty leads to turmoil. In little people, courage without Duty leads to theft and robbery."

23   Adept Kung asked: "Aren't there things the noble-minded hate?"

"Yes, there are," replied the Master. "They hate those who denounce what is hateful in others. They hate those who live poor and revile the privileged. They hate those who honor courage and neglect Ritual. And they hate those who are impetuous and yet frustrated."

Then Kung asked: "And aren't there things you hate?"

"I hate those who mistake secondhand knowledge for wisdom," offered Kung. "I hate those who mistake audacity for courage. And I hate those who mistake gossip for honest candor."

24   The Master said: "It's women and small-minded men that are impossible to nurture. If you're close and familiar with them, they lose all humility. If you keep your distance, they're full of resentment."

25   The Master said: "If you reach forty and find it all hateful, you'll be that way to the death."

士　是　逗　興　顗　月
仁　拊　禮　立　氏　
閒　玄　器　孔　聖　寶
君　汙　　　念　　
同　以　樂　真　　希
穆　　　　　　　元
敬　水　普　世　魯
　　濟　祷　禮　親　百
　　　　鍾　樂　里　不
思　　　齊　陵　弄　改
　　　　建　遲　官

XVIII   The Lord of Wei

1　　The Lord of Wei fled the Tyrant Chou.[1] The Lord of Chi became his slave. Pi Kan tried to advise him and was put to death.

Confucius said: "In them, the Shang had three men of great Humanity."

2　　When Liu-hsia Hui was Chief Judge, he was dismissed three times. People said: "Why haven't you gone somewhere else, master?"

"If I follow the straight Way in serving people," replied Hui, "where could I go that I wouldn't be dismissed three times? If I follow a twisty Way in serving people, why should I leave this land of my parents?"

3　　Waiting for Confucius to arrive, Duke Ching of Ch'i said: "I certainly can't honor him like a patriarch from the House of Chi. I'll receive him like a patriarch from a house greater than Meng but not so great as Chi.

Then he said: "I'm so old now, I can't see how to use his ideas."

Confucius thereupon left Ch'i.

4 **C**h'i sent a gift of singing courtesans to Lu. Lord Chi Huan[2] accepted them and held no court for three days. Confucius thereupon left Lu.

5 **A** madman of Ch'u named Convergence Crazy-Cart passed by Confucius singing:

> *"Phoenix![3] Hey, sage phoenix,*
> *how's Integrity withered away so?*
>
> *What's happened can't be changed,*
> *but the future's there to be made.*
>
> *Give it up! Give it all up!*
> *High office – these days, that's the gravest of dangers."*

Confucius stepped down from his carriage, wanting to speak with this man. But CrazyCart ignored him and hurried away, so Confucius never spoke with him.[4]

6 $\mathbf{A}$s Confucius passed by, SettledConstant and BraveSeclusion were in the field plowing together. He sent Adept Lu to ask them about the river crossing.[5]

"Who's that you're driving for?" asked SettledConstant.

"Confucius," replied Adept Lu.

"You mean Confucius of Lu?"

"Yes."

"Then he must know the river crossing well."

Adept Lu then asked BraveSeclusion, but BraveSeclusion replied, "So who are you?"

"I am Chung Yu," replied Adept Lu.

"You mean Chung Yu who follows Confucius of Lu?"

"Yes."

"It's all surging and swelling," continued BraveSeclusion. "All beneath Heaven's foundering deep, and who's going to change it? To follow a man who stays clear of one person or another – how could that ever compare with following one who stays clear of the world?"

And folding earth back over seed, he went on working without pause.

Adept Lu went back and told Confucius what had happened. The Master seemed lost in troubled thought, then said: "Flocks of birds, herds of animals – we can't go roaming with them. So who can I live with, if not these humans? It's all beneath Heaven that ignores the Way: if it didn't, I wouldn't be trying so hard to change things."

7   Adept Lu was traveling with Confucius and fell behind. Meeting an old man with a basket slung from a walking-stick over his shoulder, he asked: "Have you seen the Master pass by here?"

"Your four limbs have never known work," the old man replied, "and you can't even tell the five grains apart. Who could be your Master?"

At this, he planted his walking-stick and began pulling weeds.

Adept Lu bowed and stood by reverently. So the old man invited him to stay the night. He killed a chicken and cooked up some millet. He served dinner and introduced his two sons.

The next day, Lu caught up with the Master and told him what had happened.

"Such is the recluse," responded the Master.

Then he sent Lu back to see the man again. But when Lu got there, the old man had vanished.

"To refuse office is to ignore Duty," pronounced Adept Lu. "The obligations of youth and age cannot be abandoned.

And the Duty of rulers and officials – what would happen if that were abandoned? In such devotion to self-purification, the great bonds of human community are thrown into confusion. The noble-minded put Duty into practice: they serve in office, though they know full well this world will never put the Way into practice."

8   P‌o Yi, Shu Ch'i, Yü Chung, Yi Yi, Chu Chang, Liu-hsia Hui, Shao Lien: of these recluse scholars, the Master said: "Perhaps it's true that Po Yi and Shu Ch'i remained free of compromise and disgrace. It's said that Liu-hsia Hui and Shao Lien were compromised and disgraced, though their words were at least true to the bonds of human community and their actions true to their principles. And it's said that Yü Chung and Yi Yi lived in seclusion and gave up speech altogether, keeping themselves pure and turning exile into a position of authority.

"But I'm not like them. I have no use for the strictures of *You must. You must not.*"

9   C‌hih, Grand Music-master for banquet music, left for Ch'i. Kan, Music-master for the second course, left for Ch'u. Liao, Music-master for the third course, left for Ts'ai.

And Ch'üeh, Music-master for the fourth course, left for Ch'in.

Fang Shu, master of the drum, went to live north of the Yellow River. Wu, master of the hand-drum, went to live beyond the Han River. Yang, the Grand Music-master's deputy, and Hsiang, master of the stone chimes – they went to live beyond the sea.

10 Speaking to Duke Lu, Duke Chou said: "The noble-minded never neglect their own family, and they never give their ministers cause for resentment. Unless the crimes are huge, they never abandon those they've long trusted, and they never expect perfection from anyone."

11 The great Chou had its eight noble ones:[6] elder brothers Ta and Kua, middle brothers T'u and Hu, young brothers Yeh and Hsia, younger brothers Sui and Kua.

顏氏聖念家寓魯世親里并官

肖　賢悌帝元興百主永段

票　心真處魯禮樂陵遲

迨立禮樂之曾世待鐘磬

是抒女器以注水晉泳濟鐘

仁間君居以樂之敬水清徐思

士　羅　敬　思　凉

XIX Adept Chang

1   Adept Chang said: "Willing to give up life when seeing danger, and thinking first of Duty when seeing a chance to profit; full of reverence during sacrifices, and full of grief during mourning: Fine enough! Fine enough!"

2   Adept Chang said: "Halfhearted in embracing Integrity and capricious in trusting the Way: how can they even *have it* or *have it not?*"

3   Adept Hsia's disciples asked Adept Chang about fellowship.

"What does Adept Hsia say about it?" said Chang.

"He says *Join with those who are capable and avoid those who are not.*"

"That isn't what I've heard," replied Chang. "I've heard that the noble-minded honor the wise, but make room for everyone; that they admire the virtuous and benevolent, but pity those who fall short. If I am a person of great wisdom, how can I fail to make room for everyone? And if I am less than wise, people will avoid me, so how could I think of avoiding them?"

4   Adept Hsia said: "There are lesser Ways, and there's much to be said for them. But if you follow them very far, there's sure to be mud and mire – so the noble-minded stay clear of them."

5   Adept Hsia said: "All day knowing what is beyond you, and all month never forgetting what you've mastered – then you can indeed be called a lover of learning."

6   Adept Hsia said: "Broad learning with resolute purpose, earnest inquiry with attentive reflection on things at hand – therein lies Humanity."

7   Adept Hsia said: "To perfect the hundred crafts, artisans live in their shops. To perfect the Way, the noble-minded work tirelessly at learning."

8   Adept Hsia said: "Little people always disguise their faults with pretense."

9   Adept Hsia said: "The noble-minded have three different aspects: Seen from a distance, they're majestic. Face to face, they're genial. And when they speak, they're incisive."

10   Adept Hsia said: "When the noble-minded stand by their words, they can put the people to work. When they don't stand by their words, the people call work grinding oppression.

"When the noble-minded stand by their words, they can advise the sovereign. When they don't stand by their words, the sovereign calls their advice slander."

11   Adept Hsia said: "Keep within the bounds of great Integrity. Then, in matters of small Integrity, you needn't worry about a little coming and going."

12   Adept Yu said: "Adept Hsia's disciples are so small-minded! They're fine when it comes to dusting and sweeping, replies and rejoinders, greetings and farewells. But these are frivolous things. When it comes to the deep essentials, they don't have a clue. How can this be?"

When Adept Hsia heard this, he said: "That's crazy! Yu doesn't know what he's talking about. If you start teaching the noble-minded Way too soon, people are sick of it before they're ready to learn. It's like plants and trees: you need to gauge differences. The noble-minded Way never disappoints anyone – but still, only a great sage can embrace it right through from beginning to end."

13   Adept Hsia said: "When you're an official with free time, study. When you're a student with free time, take office."

14   Adept Yu said: "In mourning – grieve fully, and then stop."

15   Adept Yu said: "My friend Adept Chang can master the most difficult things, but he still hasn't mastered Humanity."

16   Master Tseng said: "Chang is great and venerable indeed: it's impossible to work beside him cultivating Humanity."

17   Master Tseng said: "I once heard the Master say *If you haven't yet faced yourself, you will when the time comes to mourn your parents.*"

18   Master Tseng said: "I once heard the Master say *Lord Meng Chuang's filial piety might be equaled in many ways. But leaving his father's policies and advisors unchanged – that seems beyond compare.*"

19   When Yang Fu was appointed judge by the House of Meng, he went to Master Tseng for advice. Master Tseng said: "Our leaders lost the Way long ago, abandoning

the people to ruin. So don't feel happy when you manage to untangle the facts of a case; grieve in sympathy for everyone involved."

20 Adept Kung said: "Even Tyrant Chou wasn't as depraved as he's made out to be. So it is that the noble-minded keep to the high ground: everything hateful on earth flows back down to low places."

21 Adept Kung said: "Mistakes of the noble-minded are like eclipses of sun and moon: they make a mistake, and it's there for everyone to see; they make it right, and everyone looks up in awe."

22 Kung-sun Ch'ao of Wei asked Adept Kung: "Where did Confucius acquire such learning?"

"The Way of Emperors Wen and Wu never fell into ruins," replied Kung. "It abides in the people. The sage sees that greatness; others see only smallness. Something of the Way is there in everyone, so where could Confucius go without learning of it? And why would he spend years studying with some master teacher?"

23   Speaking with the ministers at court, Shu-sun Wu-shu[1] said: "Adept Kung is a greater sage than Confucius."

When Tzu-fu Ching-po reported this to him, Adept Kung said: "It's like courtyard walls. Mine stand shoulder-height, so people can look over and see how lovely the house is. But the Master's wall is fifteen or twenty feet high. Unless they're admitted through the gate, people never see the beauty of his temple and the splendor of his hundred rooms. And those who are admitted are very few indeed. So it makes perfect sense for your master to say that, doesn't it?"

24   Shu-sun Wu-shu was speaking ill of Confucius. Adept Kung said: "It's no use. There's nothing bad to say about Confucius. Others are certainly wise, but they're like mounds and hillocks, easy to scale. Confucius is like the sun and moon. How could anyone scale such heights?

"People may choose to live in darkness, but sun and moon suffer no harm. And the folly of it all is apparent to everyone."

²⁵ Adept Ch'in said to Adept Kung: "It's just your reverent humility. How can Confucius be a greater sage than you?"

"The noble-minded reveal their wisdom in a single word," replied Kung, "and in a single word they reveal their ignorance. So you can't afford to speak carelessly.

"Now, we can't reach Confucius any more than we can reach Heaven: you can't just climb a set of stairs into the sky. If Confucius were in charge of a country or noble house, it would be like the saying: *He raised them up and they stood; he showed them the Way and they set out; he offered them peace and they came; he roused them and they carried through in harmony.* He was exalted in life and mourned deeply in death. So how could we ever reach him?"

月　顗　昊　迉　是　□
元　氏　尤　立　抒　仁
□　聖　心　禮　玄　聞
　　嬰　念　器　浮　君
韋　家　真　樂　以　同
元　宮　虖　之　注　攉
　　魯　世　普　水　敬
百　親　禮　衍　済　□
王　里　樂　鍾　海　其
不改　官　遅　磬　陵　□

xx   Emperor Yao Said

Emperor Yao said:

"O Shun—
Heaven has passed its throne on to you now.

Hold fast to the middle way:
If you let this land of the four seas
fall into poverty and desperation,
the gift of Heaven is lost forever."

And in passing the throne on to Yü, Shun administered this same charge.

Emperor T'ang said: "I, your little child, dare to offer a dusky bull and call out to you, O most august and majestic Lord. You dare not pardon those who commit offense, and we servants can hide nothing from you: we are revealed in your heart. But if I commit offense, blame not the people of my ten thousand districts. And if the ten thousand districts commit offense, the blame is mine alone."

Emperor Wu knew great bounty, and so virtuous people flourished. He said:

Though I have my own family,
the Humane are beyond compare.

If the people ever transgress,
let the fault be mine alone.[1]

Pay close attention to weights and measures, re-examine laws and statutes, restore neglected offices and ministries – then the four regions will be well-governed.

Renew ravaged states, re-establish lines of succession, raise up all those who have gone into hiding – then, throughout all beneath Heaven, the people will cherish you once again in their hearts.

Matters of great weight and importance: the people, food, mourning, sacrifice.

Broad-minded, and so winning over the people; sincere, and so trusted; diligent, and so accomplishing much; fair, and so fostering joy.

2   Adept Chang asked Confucius: "What makes a person fit to govern?"

"Honoring the five graces and despising the four deformities," replied the Master, "that's what makes a person fit to govern."

"What are the five graces?" asked Adept Chang.

"The noble-minded are generous without expense, hardworking without resentment, wishful without greed, stately without arrogance, stern without cruelty."

"What is *generous without expense*?" asked Chang.

"To reward people with the rewards due them," said the Master, "is that not *generous without expense*?

"If you work people hard, but always according to their ability, how can anyone resent you? If you wish for Humanity and Humanity is realized, how is that greed? The noble-minded scorn neither the many nor the few, the humble nor the great: is that not *stately without arrogance*? The noble-minded are exacting in their dress and exalted in their gaze, so people look up to their majesty in awe: is that not *stern without cruelty*?"

"And what are the four deformities?" asked Chang.

"Killing instead of teaching, which is called terror. Expecting results without telling people what you want, which is called tyranny. Issuing vague orders and expecting prompt action, which is called plunder. Grudging and miserly when giving people what they deserve, which is called officialdom."

3 The Master said: "If you don't understand destiny, you'll never be noble-minded. If you don't understand Ritual, you'll never stand firm. And if you don't understand words, you'll never understand people."

Notes

I. To Learn, and Then

1. **Master Yu:** Disciple who later became a significant teacher in the Confucian school after Confucius' death.

2   **Humanity:** See Key Terms: *Jen*.

3   **Master Tseng:** Disciple who became a significant teacher in the Confucian school after Confucius' death.

4   **stood by my words:** Typically translated as "sincerity" or "trust," *hsin* generally appears in this translation as "standing by words" to reflect the etymology so apparent visually in the two elements of its graph, where a person is shown beside words (sounds coming out of a mouth): 信

5   **Adept Hsia:** Prominent disciple who also served as a regent for the House of Chi, the most powerful of the Three Families that had usurped governmental power. (See note V.7 for definition of *regent*.)

6   **Integrity:** See Key Terms: *Te*.

7   **Adept Kung:** Prominent disciple who became a regent for the House of Chi and a successful merchant.

8   **Duty:** See Key Terms: *Yi*.

9   **as if burnished:** *The Book of Songs*, 55.

II. In Government, the Secret

1   **thoughts never twisty:** *The Book of Songs*, 297.

2   **Lord Meng Yi:** High minister in Lu and patriarch in the

House of Meng, one of the Three Families that had usurped power in Lu.

3   **Fan Ch'ih:** Disciple.

4   **Adept Yu:** Disciple and regent.

5   **Yen Hui:** Perhaps the most able of Confucius' disciples. Confucius admired his wisdom and ability above all others and grieved deeply when he died young.

6   **Duke Ai:** Titular ruler of Lu (494–468), though the Three Families had usurped power. He tried to return power to the royal house and failed.

7   **Lord Chi K'ang:** Patriarch in the House of Chi and high minister who was de facto ruler in Lu from 492 to 468.

III. Eight Rows of Dancers

1   **what can't be?:** The first of many such attacks. The reason for Confucius' outrage is that Ritual is being violated.

2   **august and majestic:** *The Book of Songs*, 282.

3   **Lin Fang:** Nothing is known about this character or just why he appears in section 6 below. Perhaps he was a novice disciple or an influential but incapable official?

4   **Jan Ch'iu:** Disciple and minister for the House of Chi.

5   **ready for color:** *The Book of Songs*, 57 (last line absent).

6   **Wang-sun Chia:** Minister in Wei.

7   **Duke Ting:** Ruler of Lu from 509 to 495, the period during which Confucius was most active in politics.

8   **Tsai Yü:** Disciple.

9   **Kuan Chung:** In the seventh century B.C.E., Duke Huan became sovereign in Ch'i by killing his brother Chiu. Kuan

Chung was initially Chiu's advisor, but afterward became a sage Prime Minister under Duke Huan. His talents turned Ch'i into a powerful and rich state, and made Huan first among the august lords.

10 **Emperor Shun:** Mythic ruler (regnant 2255–2208 B.C.E) of great sagacity during the legendary golden age of China. See Historical Table.

11 **Emperor Wu:** Sage founder of the Chou Dynasty. "Wu" means "martial," and although he was a ruler of great virtue, he gained the throne by force. Hence, Confucius' reservation. See Introduction p. xii and Historical Table.

IV. Of Villages, Humanity

1 **That same loyalty:** See Key Terms: *shu.*

V. Kung-yeh Ch'ang

1 **Kung-yeh Ch'ang:** Disciple.

2 **Nan Jung:** Disciple.

3 **Adept Chien:** Disciple and regent.

4 **Jan Yung:** Disciple and regent for the House of Chi.

5 **Ch'i-tiao K'ai:** Disciple.

6 **Adept Lu:** Prominent disciple and minister for the House of Chi. He died fighting for Chi.

7 **regent:** Frequently used term *(tsai)* indicating a chief of government appointed to administer territory controlled by the great families who had usurped power in Lu and the other nations.

8 **Wen:** *Wen* means "cultured and refined."

9   **Yen P'ing-chung:** High minister in Ch'i who survived many changes of government because of his integrity.

10   **Tsang Wen-chung:** Minister in Lu.

11   **Lord Ning Wu:** Lord Ning Wu (seventh century B.C.E.) appeared foolish when he continued serving the Wei ruler after he lost his nation, but in the end Ning Wu saved the nation.

12   **Po Yi and Shu Ch'i:** Brothers (twelfth century B.C.E.) who were heir to the throne, but they felt it would be wrong to accept it, so they refused. As a result, they lived lives of great poverty, finally dying of cold and hunger in the mountains.

VI. Jan Yung Is One Who

1   **destiny:** Destiny in ancient Chinese must be read not in the sense of a transcendental force deciding human fate, but as the inevitable evolution of things according to the principles inherent to them.

2   **Yüan Szu:** Disciple and regent. He reappears in *Chuang Tzu* as a Taoist recluse.

3   **Ch'iu . . . go wrong:** This was a very real request for recommendation, as all three of these disciples were in fact given high positions in the government of the House of Chi.

4   **Min Tzu-ch'ien:** Disciple.

5   **Jan Po-niu:** Disciple.

6   **Meng Chih-fan:** Officer in Lu.

7   **Lady Nan:** Notorious wife of Duke Ling, ruler in Wei. See note VII.3.

8   **the constant commonplace:** *Chung yung:* also the title of the Confucian classic that deals with this principle and is generally known in English as *The Doctrine of the Mean.*

9   **Yao:** Mythic ruler (regnant 2357–2255 B.C.E.) of great sagacity during the legendary golden age of China. Yao was Shun's (note III.9) predecessor. See Historical Table.

VII. Transmitting Insight, But

1   **P'eng:** This character has never been identified with any certainty.

2   **Duke Chou:** A cultural hero much admired by Confucius and Mencius, Duke Chou helped his brother, Wu, found the Chou Dynasty. He helped set up the institutions of sage government, and is traditionally credited with developing the doctrine of the Mandate of Heaven, which introduced ethics into government (see Historical Table and Introduction pp. xiv–xv).

3   **Wei ruler:** This Wei ruler was Ch'u, son of K'uai K'ui, who was the rightful heir to Duke Ling's throne. K'uai K'ui tried to kill Lady Nan (cf. VI.27), Duke Ling's notorious wife, and fled the country when he failed. After Duke Ling's death, Ch'u inherited the throne, whereupon his father raised an army and tried to reclaim the country that was rightfully his.

4   **Change:** There is a rich bit of ambiguity here, for this character *(Yi)* may be translated either as "change" or as *The Book of Change (I Ching).* The latter is the traditional reading.

5   **Lu dialect:** That is, he used the standard literary language that was employed by the intelligentsia throughout the different nations of China. This split between the classical literary language and colloquial language continued into the twentieth century.

6   **Duke She:** Sage governor of She, a territory in the state of Ch'u.

7   **Huan T'ui:** Minister of War in Sung.

8   **Wu-ma Ch'i:** Disciple and regent.

VIII. Surely T'ai Po

1   **T'ai Po:** Eldest son of Emperor T'ai, legendary predecessor of emperors Wen and Wu, the founders of the Chou Dynasty. See Historical Table.

2   **over thin ice:** *The Book of Songs*, 195.

3   **friend:** Tradition identifies this friend as Yen Hui.

4   **"Ospreys Calling":** The first song in *The Book of Songs*.

5   **Yü:** Sage emperor from China's legendary golden age, Yü (regnant 2205–2197) succeeded Shun to the throne and founded the Hsia Dynasty.

6   **Emperor Yao . . . ways of culture:** Yao is credited with teaching humankind the arts of civilization.

IX. The Master Rarely

1   **Emperor Wen:** Father of Wu, the founder of the Chou Dynasty, Wen was considered responsible for the resplendent culture of the Chou Dynasty, hence his name, which means "culture." See Introduction p. xii and Historical Table.

2   **Phoenix . . . river . . . :** Signs heralding the appearance of a sage ruler who will bring peace and benevolent rule.

3   **Yen Hui:** Confucius' finest disciple, died young.

4   **anything but good:** *The Book of Songs*, 33.

5   **so far away:** Not in the *The Book of Songs* as we know it.

X. His Native Village

1   **Chapter X:** Confucianism was eventually reduced to hollow convention and the details of ritual. There is little justification for such doctrines in the actual teachings of Confucius, so this odd chapter (and no doubt a number of other passages scattered throughout the text) seems to be an attempt by later editors to justify them.

2   *Ch'i:* The universal breath, vital energy, or life-force.

XI. Studies Begin

1   **lines about a white-jade scepter:** From *The Book of Songs*, 256:

> *Defects in a white-jade scepter*
> *can still be polished away,*
> *but for defects in your words*
> *there's nothing to be done.*

2   *se:* Stringed instrument (similar to the *ch'in*) played by literati in ancient China: predecessor to the more familiar Japanese *koto*.

3   **Adept Kao:** Disciple and regent under the House of Chi.

4   **Chi Tzu-jan:** A leader of the usurping Chi family who employed Adept Lu and Jan Ch'iu as regents.

5   **ruining someone's son:** Both by placing him in the government of the House of Chi, who were usurpers, and by taking him away from his studies.

6   **Tseng Hsi:** Master Tseng's father. See note I.3.

XII. Yen Hui

1   **Szu-ma Niu:** According to tradition, Szu-ma Niu was a disciple of Confucius who had several disreputable brothers, among them Huan T'ui, who tried to assassinate Confucius in VII.23.

2   **one part in nine:** In the traditional well-field system, each parcel of land is divided into nine plots and so looks like the character *ching*, which means well: 井. The eight outer plots in this configuration are each cultivated by one family. In addition to cultivating their own plot, the eight families cultivate the center plot jointly. This is public land, and its produce is given to the government as a tax.

3   **Maybe . . . novelty:** This passage from *The Book of Songs*, 188 seems to have been placed here through some kind of editorial error.

4   **Duke Ching:** Ruler of Ch'i (regnant 542–490).

5   **T'ang:** Founding emperor of the Shang Dynasty (1766–1122 B.C.E.). See Historical Table.

XIII. Adept Lu

1   **losing them:** Amputation of hands and feet was a common form of punishment.

2   **Integrity . . . disgrace:** *I Ching* 32.3.

XIV: Yüan Szu Asked About

1   **Yi . . . Ao . . . Yü and Chi:** These four figures come from China's legendary prehistory, dating to the third millennium B.C.E. Yü was appointed by Shun to drain away the primal floodwaters that covered the empire, thus making agriculture possible. He later succeeded Shun to the throne and founded the Hsia Dynasty. Chi, serving as Shun's Minister of Agriculture, is credited with the invention of agriculture.

2   **Meng Kung-ch'uo:** As patriarch in the House of Meng, one of the three usurping families in Lu, Meng Kung-ch'uo had great political ambitions. What is more, the state of Lu was far from being a "tiny country."

3   **Chao or Wei:** usurping families in Chin.

4   **Kung-shu Wen-tzu:** High minister in Wei.

5   **Tsang Wu-chung:** Tsang Wu-chung was accused of plotting a revolt, hence his exile. The pretext for his demand would have been that his family needed to keep up their ancestral sacrifices.

6   **Duke Huan:** See note III.8.

7   *Wen:* "cultured and refined."

8   **He trusted . . . grief:** This answer is perhaps meant ironically, for all three figures have already appeared as dubious characters in *The Analects* (V.14, VI.15, and III.13 respectively), and Lord Chi K'ang was asking because he was a usurper who also ignored the Way.

9   **Ch'en Heng:** Patriarch of the House of Ch'en, which had been growing more and more powerul in Ch'i. It was with Ch'en Heng's assassination of Duke Chien that the usurping Ch'en family took complete control of the state.

10   **Ch'ü Po-yü:** High minister in Wei. He reappears in Chapter IV of *Chuang Tzu*, where the wordplay in his name is emphasized: Sudden ElderJade.

11   **Chi Sun:** Chi family patriarch.

12   **Kung-po Liao:** Perhaps a disciple.

13   **Tzu-fu Ching-po:** High minister of integrity under the Chi family.

14   **"When it's deep . . . step across":** *The Book of Songs*, 34.

15   **Kao Tsung:** After mourning his predecessor thus, Kao Tsung became Wu Ting, a sage Shang Dynasty emperor.

XV. Duke Ling of Wei

1   **single thread . . . :** See Key Terms: *shu*.

2   **doing nothing:** This is *wu-wei* – a concept central to Taoist, and later Ch'an (Zen) Buddhist, thought. See Introduction p. xxvii.

3   **facing south:** The ceremonial position of the emperor.

4   **Shih Yü:** Like Ch'ü Po-yü below, Shih Yü was a minister in Wei.

5   **Tsang Wen-chung, Liu-hsia Hui:** Ministers in Lu a century or so before Confucius.

6   **Three Dynasties:** Hsia, Shang, and Chou Dynasties.

7   This terse, four-character passage is quite ambiguous. Two other equally important interpretations are possible: "When they're educated, the people are all alike" and "Education is for everyone of every class."

8   **Music-master Mien:** At the time, only the blind entered the musical profession.

XVI. The House of Chi

1   **Chuan-yü:** A small independent state within the borders of Lu.

2   The text for this section is defective. Perhaps Po Yi and Shu Ch'i (see note V.12.) are being given as examples of the model recluse in the previous section, or perhaps there is something missing at the beginning of this section. Also, it seems to be another statement by Confucius, but this is not indicated in the text.

XVII. Yang Huo

1   **Yang Huo:** Although nominally only regent to the House of Chi, Yang Huo wielded the family's power and eventually took control of the entire country of Lu.

2   **Wu-ch'eng:** Place governed by Adept Yu.

3   **Kung-shan Fu-jao:** A regent under the House of Chi and a confederate of Yang Huo. Confucius perhaps imagined that Yang intended to restore power to the rightful ruler of Lu.

4   **Pi Hsi:** Regent under one of the great houses in Chin.

5   ***Chou Nan* and the *Shao Nan:*** The first two chapters in *The Book of Songs.*

6   **Way:** The original meaning of Way *(Tao)* is "road."

7   **songs of Cheng . . . Ya:** Two sections in *The Book of Songs.*

XVIII. The Lord of Wei

1   **Tyrant Chou:** Last emperor of the Shang Dynasty, known for his vicious rule. His overthrow by Emperor Wu marked the beginning of the Chou Dynasty.

2   **Lord Chi Huan:** Patriarch in the House of Chi and high minister who was de facto ruler in Lu from 505 to 492.

3   **Phoenix:** See note IX.2.

4   This begins a group of sections that provide a Taoist counterbalance to Confucian doctrine. They were perhaps included by a later editor with Taoist sympathies.

    For another version of this particular story, see Chapter IV of *Chuang Tzu* (Hinton translation, p. 62).

5   **river crossing:** The river crossing can be taken literally: the implication then is that Confucius should know where it is because he spends so much time wandering around foolishly trying to save the world. But for later writers who alluded to this passage, T'ao Ch'ien for instance, the river crossing came to represent the Way through this "surging and swelling" world that a sage masters.

6   **eight noble ones:** It was said that when a dynasty truly flourished a woman would give birth to four sets of twins, all of whom would become distinguished men.

XIX. Adept Chang

    Chapter XIX: This chapter seems to involve the disciples after Confucius' death.

1   **Shu-sun Wu-shu:** Minister in Lu.

XX. Emperor Yao Said

1   **Shun . . . Yü . . . T'ang . . . Wu:** The sage-emperor Shun was the last emperor of the legendary pre-dynastic period, and so is a kind of founding patriarch to the Three Dy-

nasties. Within the Three Dynasties: Yü founded the Hsia Dynasty, T'ang founded the Shang, and Wu founded the Chou. See Historical Table.

Historical Table

Emperors

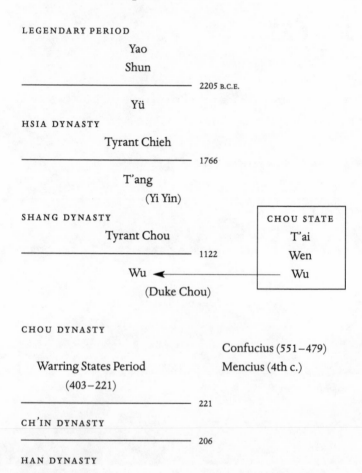

LEGENDARY PERIOD

Yao

Shun

———————————————————— 2205 B.C.E.

Yü

HSIA DYNASTY

Tyrant Chieh

———————————————————— 1766

T'ang

(Yi Yin)

SHANG DYNASTY

	CHOU STATE
Tyrant Chou	T'ai
	Wen

———————————————————— 1122

Wu ◄——————————— Wu

(Duke Chou)

CHOU DYNASTY

Confucius (551–479)

Warring States Period   Mencius (4th c.)

(403–221)

———————————————————— 221

CH'IN DYNASTY

———————————————————— 206

HAN DYNASTY

Key Terms
An Outline of Confucian Thought

Li: 禮   Ritual

A religious concept associated with the worship of gods and spirits prior to Confucius, Ritual was reconfigured by Confucius to mean the web of social responsibilities that bind a society together. These include the proprieties in virtually all social interactions, and are determined by the individual's position within the structure of society. By calling these secular acts "Ritual," Confucius makes everyday experience itself a sacred realm. This Ritual structure of society is part of a vast cosmological weave: the Ritual structure of natural process as the ten thousand things emerge from the primal emptiness.

Jen: 仁   Humanity (Humane)

The character for *jen* is formed by a combination of the characters for "human being" and "two," and it means all of the moral qualities expressed in the behavior of ideal human beings toward one another. *Jen* is the internalization of *li,* and *li* is the codified external expression of *jen.* So, to be Humane means to master a kind of selflessness by which we dwell as an integral part of the Ritual weave. Or, more simply, practicing *jen* means to act with a selfless and reverent concern for the well-being of others. *Jen* is the touchstone of Confucian sagehood, a kind of enlightenment that Confucius claimed was beyond even him.

Yi: 義 Duty

The prescriptions of Ritual are general in nature. The ability to apply them in specific situations is Duty, and so Duty is the particular ethical expression of Humanity.

Tao: 道 Way

The effortless process of human society functioning according to its natural Ritual structure. It can be expanded to cover Ritual's cosmological dimensions, making it comparable to the concept of *Tao*. Hence: the effortless process of the cosmos functioning according to its natural Ritual structure. The cosmos always abides by the Tao, with the frequent exception of human societies.

Te: 德 Integrity

The ability to act according to the Way. Or, more precisely, the embodiment of the Tao in the sage, where it becomes a kind of power through which the sage can transform others "by example."

T'ien: 天 Heaven

Natural process. Or, more descriptively, the inevitable unfolding of things in the cosmological process. Hence, Heaven appears as a kind of immanent fate in the human realm – and as Ritual is its organizing principle, it becomes a kind of moral force encouraging societies to abide by Ritual and the Tao.

Shu 恕

According to Confucius, to "never impose on others what you would not choose for yourself" (XV.24). In a word, it might be defined as "reciprocity," for its etymological meaning is something like: "as if heart," hence "treat others as if their hearts were your own." So the definition of this word is often spoken of as Confucius' "Golden Rule." In any case, when Confucius speaks of the "single thread stringing my Way together," it is identified as *chung shu:* literally "loyalty to *shu*" or "loyalty and *shu*" (IV.15). *Chung's* etymological meaning is "centered in heart," so this complex little phrase is translated here as "Be loyal to the principles of your heart, and treat others with that same loyalty."

Further Reading

Chan Wing-tsit. *A Source Book of Chinese Philosophy*. New York: Columbia University Press, 1969.

Chuang Tzu. *Chuang Tzu: The Inner Chapters*. Trans. David Hinton. Washington, D.C.: Counterpoint, 1997.

Confucius. *The Analects*. Trans. D. C. Lau. London: Penguin, 1979.

———. The Analects, Vol. I The Chinese Classics. Trans. James Legge. 1861–73. Reprint Hong Kong: University of Hong Kong Press, 1960.

———. *The Analects of Confucius*. Trans. Simon Leys. New York: Norton, 1997.

———. *The Analects of Confucius*. Trans. Arthur Waley. London: Allen and Unwin, 1938.

———. *Confucius*. Trans. Ezra Pound. New York: New Directions, 1951.

Confucius, ed. *The Book of Songs*. Trans. Arthur Waley. London: George Allen and Unwin, 1937.

Dawson, Raymond. *Confucius*. New York: Hill and Wang, 1981.

DeBary, William T., Wing-tsit Chan, and Burton Watson, eds. *Sources of Chinese Tradition*. 2 vols. New York: Columbia University Press, 1960.

Eno, Robert. *The Confucian Creation of Heaven*. New York: State University of New York Press, 1990.

Fingarette, Herbert. *Confucius: The Secular as Sacred*. New York: Harper and Row, 1972.

Fung Yu-lan. *A History of Chinese Philosophy.* Trans. Derk Bodde. Princeton: Princeton University Press, 1952–53.

Graham, A. C. *Disputers of the Tao.* LaSalle: Open Court, 1989.

Hall, David, and Roger Ames. *Thinking Through Confucius.* New York: State University of New York Press. 1987.

Hsün Tzu. *Hsün Tzu.* Trans. Burton Watson. New York: Columbia University Press, 1963.

Hughes, E. R. *The Great Learning and the Mean in Action.* London: Dent, 1942.

Mencius. *Mencius.* Trans. David Hinton. Washington, D.C.: Counterpoint, 1998.

Mote, Frederick. *Intellectual Foundations of China.* New York: Alfred A. Knopf, 1971.

Ropp, Paul, ed. *Heritage of China.* Berkeley: University of California Press, 1990.

Schwartz, Benjamin. *The World of Thought in Ancient China.* Cambridge: Harvard University Press, 1985.

Tu Wei-ming. *Humanity and Self-Cultivation: Essays in Confucian Thought.* Berkeley: Asian Humanities Press, 1979.